San Rafael Public Library
1100 E. Street
San Rafael, CA 94901

AUG - - 201
Y0-BVQ-295

THE WHO'S BUYING SERIES
BY THE NEW STRATEGIST EDITORS

Who's Buying

for Travel

10th EDITION

New Strategist Press, LLC.
P.O. Box 635, Amityville, New York 11701
800/848-0842; 631-608-8795
www.newstrategist.com

© 2014. NEW STRATEGIST PRESS, LLC.

All rights reserved.

No part of this book may be reproduced, stored in a retrieval system, or transmitted in any form
or by any means, electronic, mechanical, photocopying, microfilming, recording, or otherwise
without written permission from the Publisher.

ISBN 978-1-940308-61-6 (paper)
ISBN 978-1-940308-62-3 (e-book)

Printed in the United States of America.

Contents

Household Spending on Travel by Product Category, 2012

About the Data in *Who's Buying for Travel*

Introduction

The spending data in *Who's Buying for Travel* are based on the Bureau of Labor Statistics' Consumer Expenditure Survey, an ongoing, nationwide survey of household spending. The Consumer Expenditure Survey is a complete accounting of household expenditures. It includes everything from big-ticket items, such as homes and cars, to small purchases like laundry detergent and videos. The survey does not include expenditures by government, business, or institutions. The data in this report are from the 2012 Consumer Expenditure Survey, unless otherwise noted.

To produce this report, New Strategist Press analyzed the Consumer Expenditure Survey's average household spending data in a variety of ways, calculating household spending indexes, aggregate (or total) household spending, and market shares. This report shows spending data by age, household income, household type, race, Hispanic origin, region of residence, and education. These analyses are presented in two formats—for all product categories by demographic characteristic and for all demographic characteristics by product category.

Definition of Consumer Unit

The Consumer Expenditure Survey uses the consumer unit rather than the household as the sampling unit. The term "household" is used interchangeably with the term "consumer unit" in this report for convenience, although they are not exactly the same. Some households contain more than one consumer unit.

The Bureau of Labor Statistics defines consumer units as either: (1) members of a household who are related by blood, marriage, adoption, or other legal arrangements; (2) a person living alone or sharing a household with others or living as a roomer in a private home or lodging house or in permanent living quarters in a hotel or motel, but who is financially independent; or (3) two or more persons living together who pool their income to make joint expenditure decisions. The bureau defines financial independence in terms of "the three major expense categories: housing, food, and other living expenses. To be considered financially independent, at least two of the three major expense categories have to be provided by the respondent."

The Census Bureau uses the household as its sampling unit in the decennial census and in the monthly Current Population Survey. The Census Bureau's household "consists of all persons who occupy a housing unit. A house, an apartment or other groups of rooms, or a single room is regarded as a housing unit when it is occupied or intended for occupancy as separate living quarters; that is, when the occupants do not live and eat with any other persons in the structure and there is direct access from the outside or through a common hall."

The definition goes on to specify that "a household includes the related family members and all the unrelated persons, if any, such as lodgers, foster children, wards, or employees who share the housing unit. A person living alone in a housing unit or a group of unrelated persons sharing a housing unit as partners is also counted as a household. The count of households excludes group quarters."

Because there can be more than one consumer unit in a household, consumer units outnumber households by several million. Young adults under age 25 head most of the additional consumer units.

How to Use the Tables in This Report

The starting point for all calculations are the unpublished, detailed average household spending data collected by the Consumer Expenditure Survey. These numbers are shown on the report's average spending tables and on each of the product-specific tables. New Strategist's editors calculated the other figures in the report based on the average figures. The indexed spending tables and the indexed spending column (Best Customers) on the product-specific tables reveal whether spending by households in a given segment is above or below the average for all households and by how much. The total (or aggregate) spending tables show the overall size of the market. The market share tables and market share column (Biggest Customers) on the product-specific tables reveal how much spending each household segment controls. These analyses are described in detail below.

• **Average Spending.** The average spending figures show the average annual spending of households on travel in 2012. The Consumer Expenditure Survey produces average spending data for all households in a segment, e.g., all households with a householder aged 25 to 34, not just for those who purchased the item. When examining spending data, it is important to remember that by including both travelers and nontravelers in the calculation, the average is less than the amount spent on the item by buyers. (See Table 1 for the percentage of households that spent on travel in 2012 and how much the purchasers spent.)

Because average spending figures include both buyers and nonbuyers, they reveal spending patterns by demographic characteristic. By knowing who is most likely to spend on an item, marketers can target their advertising and promotions more efficiently, and businesses can determine the market potential of a product or service in a city or neighborhood. By multiplying the average amount households spend on airfares by the number of households in an area, for example, a newspaper could show an airline the potential size of the market in its area, convincing it to advertise to the local population.

• **Indexed Spending (Best Customers).** The indexed spending figures compare the spending of each household segment with that of the average household. To compute the indexes, New Strategist divides the average amount each household segment spends on an item by average household spending and multiplies the resulting figure by 100.

An index of 100 is the average for all households. An index of 125 means the spending of a household segment is 25 percent above average (100 plus 25). An index of 75 indicates spending that is 25 percent below the average for all households (100 minus 25). Indexed spending figures identify the best customers for a product or service. Households with an index of 178 for lodging, for example, are a strong market for this service. Those with an index below 100 are a weak market.

Spending indexes can reveal hidden markets—household segments with a high propensity to buy a particular product or service but which are overshadowed by household segments that account for a larger share of the market. Householders aged 65 to 74, for example, account for 20 percent of spending on intercity train fares, similar to the 19 percent accounted for by householders aged 45 to 54. But a look at the indexed spending figures reveals that, in fact, the older householders are the better customers. They spend 66 percent more than the average household on train fares compared with average spending (index of 96) by householders aged 45 to 54. Rail tour marketers can use this information to target their best customers.

Note that because of sampling errors, small differences in index values may be insignificant. But the broader patterns revealed by indexes can guide marketers to the best customers.

• **Total (Aggregate) Spending.** To produce the total (aggregate) spending figures, New Strategist multiplies average spending by the number of households in a segment. The result is the dollar size of the total household market and of each market segment. All totals are shown in thousands of dollars. To convert the numbers in the total spending tables to dollars, you must append "000" to the number. For example, households headed by married couples without children at home spent almost $16 billion ($15,811,364,000) on lodging in 2012.

When comparing the total spending figures in this report with total spending estimates from the Bureau of Economic Analysis, other government agencies, or trade associations, keep in mind that the Consumer Expenditure Survey includes only household spending, not spending by businesses or institutions. Sales data also differ from household spending totals because sales figures for consumer products include the value of goods sold to industries, government, and foreign markets, which may be a significant proportion of sales.

• **Market Shares (Biggest Customers).** New Strategist produces market share figures by converting total (aggregate) spending data into percentages. To calculate the percentage of total spending on an item that is controlled by each demographic segment—i.e., its market share—each segment's total spending on an item is divided by aggregate household spending on the item.

Market shares reveal the biggest customers—the demographic segments that account for the largest share of spending on a particular product or service. In 2012, for example, households headed by college graduates accounted for 66 percent of spending on airline fares, more than double their 32 percent share of consumer units. By targeting only the best-educated consumers, airlines can reach the majority of their customers. There is a danger here, however. By single-mindedly targeting the biggest customers, businesses cannot nurture potential growth markets. With competition for customers more heated than ever, targeting potential markets is increasingly important to business survival.

• **Product-Specific Tables.** The product-specific tables reveal at a glance the demographic characteristics of spending by individual product category. These tables show average spending, indexed spending (Best Customers), and market shares (Biggest Customers) by age, income, household type, race and Hispanic origin, region of residence, and education. If you want to see the spending pattern for an individual product at a glance, these are the tables for you.

History and Methodology of the Consumer Expenditure Survey

The Consumer Expenditure Survey is an ongoing study of the day-to-day spending of American households. In taking the survey, government interviewers collect spending data on products and services as well as the amount and sources of household income, changes in saving and debt, and demographic and economic characteristics of household members. The Bureau of the Census collects data for the Consumer Expenditure Survey under contract with the Bureau of Labor Statistics, which is responsible for analysis and release of the survey data.

Since the late 19th century, the federal government has conducted expenditure surveys about every 10 years. Although the results have been used for a variety of purposes, their primary application is to track consumer prices. In 1980, the Consumer Expenditure Survey became continuous with annual release of data. The survey is used to update prices for the market basket of products and services used in calculating the Consumer Price Index.

The Consumer Expenditure Survey consists of two separate surveys: an interview survey and a diary survey. In the interview portion of the survey, respondents are asked each quarter for five consecutive quarters to report their expenditures for the previous three months. The interview survey records purchases of big-ticket items such as houses, cars, and major appliances, and recurring expenses such as insurance premiums, utility payments, and rent. The interview component covers about 95 percent of all expenditures.

The diary survey records expenditures on small, frequently purchased items during a two-week period. These detailed records include expenses for food and beverages purchased in grocery stores and at restaurants, as well as other items such as tobacco, housekeeping supplies, nonprescription drugs, and personal care products and services. The diary survey is intended to capture expenditures respondents are likely to forget or recall incorrectly over longer periods of time.

Two separate, nationally representative samples are used for the interview and diary surveys. For the interview survey, about 7,000 consumer units are interviewed on a rotating panel basis each quarter for five consecutive quarters. Another 7,000 consumer units kept weekly diaries of spending for two consecutive weeks. Data collection is carried out in 91 areas of the country.

The Bureau of Labor Statistics reviews, audits, and cleanses the data, then weights them to reflect the number and characteristics of all U.S. consumer units. Like any sample survey, the Consumer Expenditure Survey is subject to two major types of error. Nonsampling error occurs when respondents misinterpret questions or interviewers are inconsistent in the way they ask questions or record answers. Respondents may forget items, recall expenses incorrectly, or deliberately give wrong answers. A respondent may remember how much he or she spent at the grocery store but forget the items picked up at a local convenience store. Mistakes during the various stages of data processing and refinement can also cause nonsampling error.

Sampling error occurs when a sample does not accurately represent the population it is supposed to represent. This kind of error is present in every sample-based survey and is minimized by using a proper sampling procedure. Standard error tables documenting the extent of sampling error in the Consumer Expenditure Survey are available from the Bureau of Labor Statistics at http://www.bls.gov/cex/csxcombined.htm.

Although the Consumer Expenditure Survey is the best source of information about the spending behavior of American households, it should be treated with caution because of the above problems.

For More Information

To find out more about the Consumer Expenditure Survey, contact the specialists at the Bureau of Labor Statistics at (202) 691-6900, or visit the Consumer Expenditure Survey home page at http://www.bls.gov/cex/. The web site includes news releases, technical documentation, and current and historical summary-level data. The detailed average spending data shown in this report are available from the Bureau of Labor Statistics only by special request.

For a comprehensive look at detailed household spending data for all products and services, see the 19th edition of *Household Spending: Who Spends How Much on What*. New Strategist's books are available in hardcopy or as downloads with links to the Excel version of each table. Find out more by visiting http://www .newstrategist.com or by calling 1-800-848-0842.

Table 1. Percent reporting expenditure and amount spent, average quarter, 2012

(percent of consumer units reporting expenditure and amount spent by purchasers during the average quarter, 2012)

	average quarter	
	percent reporting expenditure	**amount spent by purchasers**
Travel		
Admission to sports events on trips	8.3%	$45.07
Airline fares	10.7	825.98
Alcoholic beverages purchased on trips	12.7	86.15
Auto rental on trips	1.9	306.06
Bus fares, intercity	4.4	67.49
Gasoline on trips	21.1	174.91
Groceries on trips	10.4	120.86
Local transportation on trips	5.3	53.33
Lodging on trips	15.1	565.21
Luggage	1.5	112.16
Motor oil on trips	21.1	1.77
Movie, other admissions, on trips	8.3	135.29
Parking fees on trips	3.5	49.28
Participant sports on trips	3.5	191.35
Recreation expenses on trips	7.6	69.32
Restaurants and carry-outs on trips	24.6	260.91
Ship fares	2.1	666.63
Taxi fares and limousine services on trips	5.3	31.32
Tolls on trips	6.7	16.62
Train fares, intercity	4.3	109.01
Truck rental on trips	0.1	291.07

Source: Calculations by New Strategist based on the Bureau of Labor Statistics' 2012 Consumer Expenditure Survey

Household Spending Trends, 2000 to 2012

Household spending declined during the Great Recession and its aftermath, bottoming out in 2010. Then things began to get better. Between 2010 and 2012, average annual household spending climbed 1.6 percent to $51,442, after adjusting for inflation. The 2012 figure was still 6.7 percent below the 2006 peak, however, when the average household spent $55,118.

Although household spending is growing again, the average household is spending less than it did in 2006 on most items. Spending on alcoholic beverages is an example. Although the average household spent 4 percent more on alcoholic beverages in 2012 ($451) than in 2010 ($434), the 2012 figure is 20 percent below the 2006 figure ($566). Many categories show a similar pattern. The average household spent 5 percent more on furniture in 2012 ($391) than in 2010 ($374), but the amount spent by the average household on furniture in 2012 was 26 percent below the spending of 2006 ($527). Spending on new cars and trucks increased by a substantial 28 percent between 2010 and 2012, but the 2012 figure was still 20 percent below the level of 2006.

Other categories continued their decline in the 2010-to-2012 time period, despite the overall spending recovery. Average household spending on mortgage interest fell 13 percent between 2010 and 2012, after adjusting for inflation, as more Americans chose to rent rather than buy a home. Spending on apparel continued its long-term decline. Conversely, a handful of spending categories have grown steadily despite the Great Recession, including health insurance, medical services, education, and the category "pets, toys, and playground equipment" (dominated by pet spending).

Although household spending is beginning to recover from the Great Recession, the recovery is slow and spending on many categories continues to decline. But those who have been eagerly awaiting good economic news should take heart at the spending boost for items such as new cars and trucks, household textiles, reading material, footwear, personal care products and services, cash contributions, and gifts for people in other households. Americans may be starting to open their wallets, at least a bit.

Households are spending more, but still less than they once did

(percent change in spending by the average household on selected products and services, 2006, 2010, and 2012; in 2012 dollars)

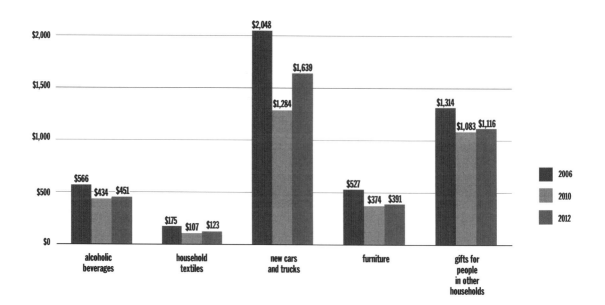

Table 2. Household spending trends, 2000 to 2012

(average annual spending of total consumer units, 2000, 2006, 2010, and 2012; percent change, 2000–06, 2006–12, and 2010–12; in 2012 dollars)

	average annual household spending (in 2012$)				percent change		
	2012	2010	2006	2000	2010–12	2006–12	2000–06
Number of consumer units (in 000s)	124,416	121,107	118,843	109,367	2.7%	4.7%	8.7%
Average annual spending of consumer units	$51,442	$50,655	$55,118	$50,725	1.6	–6.7	8.7
FOOD	6,599	6,453	6,960	6,877	2.3	–5.2	1.2
Food at home	3,921	3,816	3,891	4,028	2.8	0.8	–3.4
Cereals and bakery products	538	529	508	604	1.8	5.9	–15.9
Cereals and cereal products	182	174	163	208	4.8	11.8	–21.7
Bakery products	356	355	346	396	0.3	2.8	–12.6
Meats, poultry, fish, and eggs	852	825	908	1,060	3.2	–6.1	–14.4
Beef	226	228	269	317	–1.1	–15.9	–15.3
Pork	166	157	179	223	5.8	–7.2	–19.7
Other meats	122	123	120	135	–1.0	2.0	–11.2
Poultry	159	145	161	193	9.4	–1.0	–16.9
Fish and seafood	126	123	139	147	2.3	–9.3	–5.3
Eggs	53	48	42	45	9.4	25.8	–7.0
Dairy products	419	400	419	433	4.7	0.0	–3.3
Fresh milk and cream	152	148	159	175	2.4	–4.7	–8.7
Other dairy products	267	253	260	257	5.7	2.8	0.9
Fruits and vegetables	731	715	674	695	2.2	8.4	–2.9
Fresh fruits	261	244	222	217	6.8	17.5	2.2
Fresh vegetables	226	221	220	212	2.2	2.8	3.7
Processed fruits	114	119	124	153	–4.2	–8.2	–19.0
Processed vegetables	130	131	108	112	–0.4	20.2	–3.4
Other food at home	1,380	1,346	1,380	1,236	2.6	0.0	11.7
Sugar and other sweets	147	139	142	156	5.8	3.3	–8.7
Fats and oils	114	108	98	111	5.1	16.4	–11.5
Miscellaneous foods	699	702	714	583	–0.5	–2.1	22.6
Nonalcoholic beverages	370	351	378	333	5.5	–2.1	13.4
Food prepared by consumer unit on trips	50	45	49	53	10.4	2.1	–8.2
Food away from home	2,678	2,638	3,068	2,849	1.5	–12.7	7.7
ALCOHOLIC BEVERAGES	451	434	566	496	4.0	–20.3	14.1
HOUSING	16,887	17,433	18,639	16,425	–3.1	–9.4	13.5
Shelter	9,891	10,331	11,016	9,485	–4.3	–10.2	16.1
Owned dwellings	6,056	6,609	7,421	6,136	–8.4	–18.4	20.9
Mortgage interest and charges	3,067	3,528	4,274	3,519	–13.1	–28.2	21.5
Property taxes	1,836	1,910	1,878	1,519	–3.9	–2.2	23.7
Maintenance, repair, insurance, other expenses	1,153	1,171	1,270	1,100	–1.5	–9.2	15.4
Rented dwellings	3,186	3,053	2,950	2,712	4.3	8.0	8.8
Other lodging	649	669	646	637	–2.9	0.5	1.3
Utilities, fuels, and public services	3,648	3,854	3,869	3,319	–5.3	–5.7	16.6
Natural gas	359	463	580	409	–22.5	–38.1	41.6
Electricity	1,388	1,488	1,442	1,215	–6.7	–3.7	18.7
Fuel oil and other fuels	137	147	157	129	–7.1	–12.8	21.5
Telephone services	1,239	1,240	1,238	1,169	–0.1	0.1	5.9
Water and other public services	525	515	452	395	2.0	16.1	14.6
Household services	1,159	1,060	1,080	912	9.3	7.4	18.4
Personal services	368	358	448	435	2.8	–17.8	3.0
Other household services	791	702	632	477	12.6	25.1	32.4
Housekeeping supplies	610	644	729	643	–5.3	–16.3	13.4
Laundry and cleaning supplies	155	158	172	175	–1.9	–9.9	–1.5
Other household products	319	346	376	301	–7.9	–15.1	24.7
Postage and stationery	136	139	181	168	–2.1	–24.9	7.8
Household furnishings and equipment	1,580	1,545	1,945	2,065	2.3	–18.8	–5.8
Household textiles	123	107	175	141	14.5	–29.9	24.1
Furniture	391	374	527	521	4.6	–25.8	1.1
Floor coverings	16	38	55	59	–57.8	–70.7	–6.8
Major appliances	197	220	274	252	–10.5	–28.2	8.9
Small appliances and miscellaneous housewares	98	113	124	116	–13.0	–21.1	7.0
Miscellaneous household equipment	754	692	789	975	9.0	–4.5	–19.0

	average annual household spending (in 2012$)				percent change		
	2012	2010	2006	2000	2010–12	2006–12	2000–06
APPAREL AND RELATED SERVICES	**$1,736**	**$1,790**	**$2,134**	**$2,475**	**–3.0%**	**–18.7%**	**–13.8%**
Men and boys	**408**	**402**	**506**	**587**	**1.4**	**–19.3**	**–13.8**
Men, aged 16 or older	320	320	402	459	0.0	–20.4	–12.3
Boys, aged 2 to 15	88	82	104	128	7.1	–15.1	–19.0
Women and girls	**688**	**698**	**855**	**967**	**–1.4**	**–19.6**	**–11.5**
Women, aged 16 or older	573	592	716	809	–3.2	–20.0	–11.5
Girls, aged 2 to 15	116	106	139	157	9.1	–16.5	–11.7
Children under age 2	**63**	**96**	**109**	**109**	**–34.2**	**–42.4**	**0.0**
Footwear	**347**	**319**	**346**	**457**	**8.8**	**0.2**	**–24.3**
Other apparel products and services	**230**	**275**	**319**	**355**	**–16.3**	**–27.9**	**–10.1**
TRANSPORTATION	**8,998**	**8,083**	**9,689**	**9,889**	**11.3**	**–7.1**	**–2.0**
Vehicle purchases	**3,210**	**2,725**	**3,896**	**4,557**	**17.8**	**–17.6**	**–14.5**
Cars and trucks, new	1,639	1,284	2,048	2,140	27.7	–20.0	–4.3
Cars and trucks, used	1,516	1,388	1,786	2,360	9.2	–15.1	–24.3
Gasoline and motor oil	**2,756**	**2,245**	**2,536**	**1,721**	**22.8**	**8.7**	**47.3**
Other vehicle expenses	**2,490**	**2,594**	**2,682**	**3,041**	**–4.0**	**–7.2**	**–11.8**
Vehicle finance charges	223	256	339	437	–12.8	–34.3	–22.4
Maintenance and repairs	814	829	784	832	–1.8	3.9	–5.8
Vehicle insurance	1,018	1,063	1,009	1,037	–4.3	0.9	–2.7
Vehicle rentals, leases, licenses, other charges	434	445	549	735	–2.6	–20.9	–25.3
Public transportation	**542**	**519**	**575**	**569**	**4.4**	**–5.8**	**1.0**
HEALTH CARE	**3,556**	**3,324**	**3,150**	**2,755**	**7.0**	**12.9**	**14.4**
Health insurance	2,061	1,928	1,668	1,311	6.9	23.5	27.3
Medical services	839	760	763	757	10.4	10.0	0.8
Drugs	515	511	585	555	0.8	–12.0	5.5
Medical supplies	142	125	133	132	13.3	6.6	0.9
ENTERTAINMENT	**2,605**	**2,637**	**2,706**	**2,484**	**–1.2**	**–3.7**	**8.9**
Fees and admissions	614	612	690	687	0.4	–11.0	0.5
Audio and visual equipment and services	979	1,004	1,032	829	–2.5	–5.1	24.4
Pets, toys, and playground equipment	648	638	469	445	1.6	38.1	5.4
Other entertainment products and services	363	383	514	524	–5.3	–29.3	–2.0
PERSONAL CARE PRODUCTS AND SERVICES	**628**	**613**	**666**	**752**	**2.5**	**–5.7**	**–11.4**
READING	**109**	**105**	**133**	**195**	**3.5**	**–18.2**	**–31.5**
EDUCATION	**1,207**	**1,131**	**1,011**	**843**	**6.7**	**19.4**	**20.0**
TOBACCO PRODUCTS AND SMOKING SUPPLIES	**332**	**381**	**372**	**425**	**–12.9**	**–10.9**	**–12.4**
MISCELLANEOUS	**829**	**894**	**963**	**1,035**	**–7.3**	**–14.0**	**–6.9**
CASH CONTRIBUTIONS	**1,913**	**1,719**	**2,129**	**1,589**	**11.3**	**10.1**	**33.9**
PERSONAL INSURANCE AND PENSIONS	**5,591**	**5,657**	**6,002**	**4,487**	**–1.2**	**–6.8**	**33.8**
Life and other personal insurance	353	335	367	532	5.4	–3.7	–31.1
Pensions and Social Security*	5,238	5,321	5,635	3,955	–1.6	–7.0	*
PERSONAL TAXES	**2,226**	**1,863**	**2,770**	**4,156**	**19.5**	**–19.6**	**–33.4**
Federal income taxes	1,568	1,196	1,949	3,212	31.1	–19.5	–39.3
State and local income taxes	526	508	591	749	3.6	–11.0	–21.1
Other taxes	132	159	230	195	–17.0	–42.6	18.2
GIFTS FOR PEOPLE IN OTHER HOUSEHOLDS	**1,116**	**1,083**	**1,314**	**1,444**	**3.0**	**–15.1**	**–9.0**

*Recent spending on pensions and Social Security is not comparable with 2000 because of changes in methodology.
Note: Spending by category does not add to total spending because gift spending is also included in the preceding product and service categories and personal taxes are not included in the total.
Source: Bureau of Labor Statistics, 2000, 2006, 2010, and 2012 Consumer Expenditure Surveys, Internet site http://www.bls.gov/cex/; calculations by New Strategist

Household Spending on Travel, 2000 to 2012

Travel is one of the most popular leisure-time activities. In 2012, the average household spent $1,478 on travel, including airline fares, lodging, luggage, meals, and recreational expenses. The three largest travel expense categories—airline fares, lodging, and restaurant meals—account for 64 percent of travel spending.

Average household spending on travel held essentially steady between 2000 and the overall peak spending year of 2006, after adjusting for inflation. As the Great Recession set in, spending on travel fell 14 percent between 2006 and 2010 (the overall spending trough year). From 2010 to 2012 average household spending on travel rebounded, climbing 7 percent. Despite the rebound, luggage was the only travel category for which average household spending increased appreciably during the 2006-to-2012 time period, rising by a strong 55 percent.

The travel spending recovery from 2010 to 2012 was strongest for ship fares. The average household spent 36 percent more on ship fares in 2012 than in 2010, after adjusting for inflation. Also growing strongly during the two-year period was spending on gasoline when traveling and intercity train fares. There was no improvement in spending on recreational expenses on trips, once the fourth-largest travel category.

Table 3. Travel spending, 2000 to 2012

(average annual and percent distribution of household spending on travel by category, 2000 to 2012; percent change in spending and percentage point change in distribution, 2000–06, 2006–12, and 2010–12; in 2012 dollars; ranked by amount spent)

	average annual household spending (in 2012$)				percent change		
	2012	**2010**	**2006**	**2000**	**2010–12**	**2006–12**	**2000–06**
Average household spending on travel	**$1,478.35**	**$1,375.23**	**$1,606.12**	**$1,593.93**	**7.5%**	**–8.0%**	**0.8%**
Airline fares	352.53	342.52	381.06	365.35	2.9	–7.5	4.3
Lodging on trips	341.61	314.85	365.16	335.48	8.5	–6.5	8.8
Restaurant and carry-out food on trips	257.15	234.88	276.66	288.07	9.5	–7.1	–4.0
Gasoline and motor oil on trips	148.97	125.49	146.81	123.62	18.7	1.5	18.8
Recreational expenses on trips	128.49	128.24	168.44	194.59	0.2	–23.7	–13.4
Ship fares	56.53	41.42	62.66	48.77	36.5	–9.8	28.5
Groceries on trips	50.23	45.65	48.85	53.25	10.0	2.8	–8.3
Alcoholic beverages on trips	43.80	44.97	49.38	45.65	–2.6	–11.3	8.2
Vehicle rentals on trips	25.38	26.95	31.42	45.77	–5.8	–19.2	–31.4
Train fares, intercity	18.88	16.50	18.55	28.16	14.4	1.8	–34.1
Local transportation on trips	17.81	17.75	23.73	22.56	0.3	–25.0	5.2
Luggage	13.79	13.31	8.92	11.09	3.6	54.6	–19.6
Bus fares, intercity	11.96	10.89	12.90	21.47	9.9	–7.3	–39.9
Parking fees and tolls on trips	11.22	11.79	11.57	10.08	–4.9	–3.0	14.8

					percentage point change		
PERCENT DISTRIBUTION OF SPENDING					**2010–12**	**2006–12**	**2000–06**
Average household spending on travel	**100.0%**	**100.0%**	**100.0%**	**100.0%**	–	–	–
Airline fares	23.8	24.9	23.7	22.9	–1.1	0.1	0.8
Lodging on trips	23.1	22.9	22.7	21.0	0.2	0.4	1.7
Restaurant and carry–out food on trips	17.4	17.1	17.2	18.1	0.3	0.2	–0.8
Gasoline and motor oil on trips	10.1	9.1	9.1	7.8	1.0	0.9	1.4
Recreational expenses on trips	8.7	9.3	10.5	12.2	–0.6	–1.8	–1.7
Ship fares	3.8	3.0	3.9	3.1	0.8	–0.1	0.8
Groceries on trips	3.4	3.3	3.0	3.3	0.1	0.4	–0.3
Alcoholic beverages on trips	3.0	3.3	3.1	2.9	–0.3	–0.1	0.2
Vehicle rentals on trips	1.7	2.0	2.0	2.9	–0.2	–0.2	–0.9
Train fares, intercity	1.3	1.2	1.2	1.8	0.1	0.1	–0.6
Local transportation on trips	1.2	1.3	1.5	1.4	–0.1	–0.3	0.1
Luggage	0.9	1.0	0.6	0.7	0.0	0.4	–0.1
Bus fares, intercity	0.8	0.8	0.8	1.3	0.0	0.0	–0.5
Parking fees and tolls on trips	0.8	0.9	0.7	0.6	–0.1	0.0	0.1

Note: Percentage point change calculations are based on unrounded figures. "–" means not applicable.
Source: Bureau of Labor Statistics, 2000, 2006, 2010, and 2012 Consumer Expenditure Surveys; calculations by New Strategist

Household Spending on Travel by Demographic Characteristic, 2012

Spending by Age

The best customers of travel are older Americans. Householders aged 55 to 64 spend the most on travel—31 percent more than the average household. Spending on travel by 55-to-64-year-olds exceeds that of other age groups in most travel categories, but there are exceptions. Householders aged 35 to 44 spend the most on luggage, and those aged 65 to 74 are the biggest spenders on bus and train fares as well as lodging and groceries on trips. Householders under age 35 and those aged 75 or older spend well below average on most travel items.

Spending by Household Income

Not surprisingly, high-income households spend far more than the average household on travel. Households with incomes of $100,000 or more accounted for half of all travel spending in 2012. High-income households spend well more than the average household on every travel category. The gap is smallest for gasoline on trips. Spending on travel is below average among householders with incomes below $70,000.

Spending by Household Type

By household type, married couples without children at home, most of them empty-nesters, are the biggest spenders on travel. Couples without children at home spend 69 percent more than average household on travel and account for 35 percent of total travel spending. The second biggest spenders on travel, married couples with school-aged children, spend 54 percent more than average. Single parents and people who live alone spend about half the average amount on travel.

Spending by Race and Hispanic Origin

Asians, who have higher incomes than other racial or ethnic groups, are by far the biggest spenders on travel. Asians spend 64 percent more than the average household on travel. In contrast, black and Hispanic households spend less than half the average amount. Asians spend more than average in all but three travel categories—luggage, gasoline, and alcoholic beverages. Their spending on airline fares is almost three times the average.

Spending by Region

Households in the West spend the most on travel—25 percent more than the average household. Households in the South spend 17 percent less than average on travel, the least among regions. While Southerners spend less than average on all travel categories, households in the West spend more than average on every travel category except for two: luggage and parking and tolls on trips. Westerners spend 38 percent more on airfares, 32 percent more on recreational expenses, and 31 percent more on groceries on trips. Households in the Northeast spend 56 percent more than average on parking fees and tolls while on trips and 54 percent more on ship fares.

Spending by Education

Travel spending rises with educational attainment because income rises with education. Only 32 percent of the nation's households are headed by people with a bachelor's degree, but they control 61 percent of travel spending. They account for the majority of spending in most travel categories, including 71 percent of train fares and 66 percent of airline fares. The share of travel spending controlled by college graduates is lowest for luggage (46 percent) and gasoline (49 percent).

Table 4. Travel: Average spending by age, 2012

(average annual spending of consumer units on travel, by age of consumer unit reference person, 2012)

	total consumer units	under 25	25 to 34	35 to 44	45 to 54	55 to 64	65 to 74	75+
Number of consumer units (in 000s)	124,416	8,159	20,112	21,598	24,624	22,770	14,993	12,161
Number of persons per consumer unit	2.5	2.0	2.8	3.4	2.7	2.1	1.8	1.5
Average before-tax income of consumer units	$65,596.00	$36,639.00	$58,832.00	$78,169.00	$81,704.00	$77,507.00	$53,521.00	$33,853.00
Average spending of consumer units, total	51,441.87	31,411.08	49,543.74	58,069.31	62,102.54	55,636.31	45,967.87	33,529.54
TRAVEL	1,478.35	522.93	1,221.95	1,414.86	1,789.97	1,931.86	1,746.49	844.93
Airline fares	352.53	157.82	299.42	328.25	433.37	463.30	386.59	200.99
Alcoholic beverages purchased on trips	43.80	22.58	49.77	44.83	48.53	52.39	43.50	21.08
Bus fares, intercity	11.96	5.94	9.10	9.97	13.28	14.45	17.31	10.37
Gasoline and motor oil on trips	148.97	74.71	146.97	155.27	167.28	176.77	170.19	75.58
Groceries on trips	50.23	8.36	39.51	47.04	66.42	64.15	65.21	24.43
Lodging on trips	341.61	83.10	246.44	317.22	427.72	438.71	460.65	212.82
Luggage	13.79	6.95	16.36	20.35	14.51	18.36	4.02	4.20
Parking fees and tolls on trips	11.22	4.44	9.97	11.22	12.73	16.00	12.41	4.30
Recreational expenses on trips	128.49	42.60	108.94	136.18	170.70	165.60	128.87	49.31
Restaurants and carry-outs on trips	257.15	83.51	220.41	243.65	316.16	334.87	302.48	137.46
Ship fares	56.53	13.45	29.30	44.98	49.37	97.58	77.27	63.03
Taxis and local transportation on trips	17.81	6.94	14.84	15.02	20.40	24.81	22.72	10.57
Train fares, intercity	18.88	6.32	13.05	15.08	18.04	25.04	31.29	18.55
Vehicle rental on trips	25.38	6.21	17.87	25.80	31.46	39.83	23.98	12.24

Source: Bureau of Labor Statistics, unpublished tables from the 2012 Consumer Expenditure Survey; calculations by New Strategist

Table 5. Travel: Indexed spending by age, 2012

(indexed average annual spending of consumer units on travel by age of consumer unit reference person, 2012; index definition: an index of 100 is the average for all consumer units; an index of 125 means that spending by consumer units in that group is 25 percent above the average for all consumer units; an index of 75 indicates spending that is 25 percent below the average for all consumer units)

	total consumer units	under 25	25 to 34	35 to 44	45 to 54	55 to 64	65 to 74	75+
Average spending of consumer units, total	**$51,442**	**$31,411**	**$49,544**	**$58,069**	**$62,103**	**$55,636**	**$45,968**	**$33,530**
Average spending of consumer units, index	**100**	**61**	**96**	**113**	**121**	**108**	**89**	**65**
TRAVEL	**100**	**35**	**83**	**96**	**121**	**131**	**118**	**57**
Airline fares	100	45	85	93	123	131	110	57
Alcoholic beverages purchased on trips	100	52	114	102	111	120	99	48
Bus fares, intercity	100	50	76	83	111	121	145	87
Gasoline and motor oil on trips	100	50	99	104	112	119	114	51
Groceries on trips	100	17	79	94	132	128	130	49
Lodging on trips	100	24	72	93	125	128	135	62
Luggage	100	50	119	148	105	133	29	30
Parking fees and tolls on trips	100	40	89	100	113	143	111	38
Recreational expenses on trips	100	33	85	106	133	129	100	38
Restaurants and carry-outs on trips	100	32	86	95	123	130	118	53
Ship fares	100	24	52	80	87	173	137	111
Taxis and local transportation on trips	100	39	83	84	115	139	128	59
Train fares, intercity	100	33	69	80	96	133	166	98
Vehicle rental on trips	100	24	70	102	124	157	94	48

Source: Calculations by New Strategist based on the Bureau of Labor Statistics' 2012 Consumer Expenditure Survey

Table 6. Travel: Total spending by age, 2012

(total annual spending on travel, by consumer unit age group, 2012; consumer units and dollars in thousands)

	total consumer units	under 25	25 to 34	35 to 44	45 to 54	55 to 64	65 to 74	75+
Number of consumer units	124,416	8,159	20,112	21,598	24,624	22,770	14,993	12,161
Total spending of all consumer units	$6,400,191,698	$256,283,002	$996,423,699	$1,254,180,957	$1,529,212,945	$1,266,838,779	$689,196,275	$407,752,736
TRAVEL	183,930,394	4,266,586	24,575,858	30,558,146	44,076,221	43,988,452	26,185,125	10,275,194
Airline fares	43,860,372	1,287,653	6,021,935	7,089,544	10,671,303	10,549,341	5,796,144	2,444,239
Alcoholic beverages purchased on trips	5,449,421	184,230	1,000,974	968,238	1,195,003	1,192,920	652,196	256,354
Bus fares, intercity	1,488,015	48,464	183,019	215,332	327,007	329,027	259,529	126,110
Gasoline and motor oil on trips	18,534,252	609,559	2,955,861	3,353,521	4,119,103	4,025,053	2,551,659	919,128
Groceries on trips	6,249,416	68,209	794,625	1,015,970	1,635,526	1,460,696	977,694	297,093
Lodging on trips	42,501,750	678,013	4,956,401	6,851,318	10,532,177	9,989,427	6,906,525	2,588,104
Luggage	1,715,697	56,705	329,032	439,519	357,294	418,057	60,272	51,076
Parking fees and tolls on trips	1,395,948	36,226	200,517	242,330	313,464	364,320	186,063	52,292
Recreational expenses on trips	15,986,212	347,573	2,191,001	2,941,216	4,203,317	3,770,712	1,932,148	599,659
Restaurants and carry-outs on trips	31,993,574	681,358	4,432,886	5,262,353	7,785,124	7,624,990	4,535,083	1,671,651
Ship fares	7,033,236	109,739	589,282	971,478	1,215,687	2,221,897	1,158,509	766,508
Taxis and local transportation on trips	2,215,849	56,623	298,462	324,402	502,330	564,924	340,641	128,542
Train fares, intercity	2,348,974	51,565	262,462	325,698	444,217	570,161	469,131	225,587
Vehicle rental on trips	3,157,678	50,667	359,401	557,228	774,671	906,929	359,532	148,851

Note: Numbers may not add to total because of rounding.
Source: Calculations by New Strategist based on the Bureau of Labor Statistics' 2012 Consumer Expenditure Survey

Table 7. Travel: Market shares by age, 2012

(percentage of total annual spending on travel accounted for by consumer unit age groups, 2012)

	total consumer units	under 25	25 to 34	35 to 44	45 to 54	55 to 64	65 to 74	75+
Share of total consumer units	**100.0%**	**6.6%**	**16.2%**	**17.4%**	**19.8%**	**18.3%**	**12.1%**	**9.8%**
Share of total before-tax income	**100.0**	**3.7**	**14.5**	**20.7**	**24.7**	**21.6**	**9.8**	**5.0**
Share of total spending	**100.0**	**4.0**	**15.6**	**19.6**	**23.9**	**19.8**	**10.8**	**6.4**
TRAVEL	**100.0**	**2.3**	**13.4**	**16.6**	**24.0**	**23.9**	**14.2**	**5.6**
Airline fares	100.0	2.9	13.7	16.2	24.3	24.1	13.2	5.6
Alcoholic beverages purchased on trips	100.0	3.4	18.4	17.8	21.9	21.9	12.0	4.7
Bus fares, intercity	100.0	3.3	12.3	14.5	22.0	22.1	17.4	8.5
Gasoline and motor oil on trips	100.0	3.3	15.9	18.1	22.2	21.7	13.8	5.0
Groceries on trips	100.0	1.1	12.7	16.3	26.2	23.4	15.6	4.8
Lodging on tripsa	100.0	1.6	11.7	16.1	24.8	23.5	16.2	6.1
Luggage	100.0	3.3	19.2	25.6	20.8	24.4	3.5	3.0
Parking fees and tolls on trips	100.0	2.6	14.4	17.4	22.5	26.1	13.3	3.7
Recreational expenses on trips	100.0	2.2	13.7	18.4	26.3	23.6	12.1	3.8
Restaurants and carry-outs on trips	100.0	2.1	13.9	16.4	24.3	23.8	14.2	5.2
Ship fares	100.0	1.6	8.4	13.8	17.3	31.6	16.5	10.9
Taxis and local transportation on trips	100.0	2.6	13.5	14.6	22.7	25.5	15.4	5.8
Train fares, intercity	100.0	2.2	11.2	13.9	18.9	24.3	20.0	9.6
Vehicle rental on trips	100.0	1.6	11.4	17.6	24.5	28.7	11.4	4.7

Note: Numbers may not add to total because of rounding.
Source: Calculations by New Strategist based on the Bureau of Labor Statistics' 2012 Consumer Expenditure Survey

Table 8. Travel: Average spending by income, 2012

(average annual spending on travel, by before-tax income of consumer units, 2012)

	total consumer units	under $20,000	$20,000–$39,999	$40,000–$49,999	$50,000–$69,999	$70,000–$79,999	$80,000–$99,999	$100,000 or more
Number of consumer units (in 000s)	124,416	26,177	28,041	11,010	17,972	6,946	10,977	23,293
Number of persons per consumer unit	2.5	1.8	2.2	2.5	2.6	2.8	2.9	3.2
Average before-tax income of consumer units	$65,596.00	$10,445.26	$29,593.01	$44,759.00	$59,283.00	$74,689.00	$88,974.00	$171,910.00
Average spending of consumer units, total	51,441.87	22,404.57	33,454.51	41,567.34	49,981.57	59,984.14	67,417.91	101,422.59
TRAVEL	**1,478.35**	**385.89**	**623.10**	**869.77**	**1,213.40**	**1,661.81**	**2,012.95**	**3,922.91**
Airline fares	352.53	95.67	140.67	194.06	305.61	363.05	426.10	969.51
Alcoholic beverages purchased on trips	43.80	10.62	14.22	27.11	36.90	42.62	68.80	118.51
Bus fares, intercity	11.96	6.29	7.03	6.91	12.90	13.80	17.17	22.95
Gasoline and motor oil on trips	148.97	49.34	93.53	119.34	152.37	211.58	243.86	275.65
Groceries on trips	50.23	15.50	27.90	33.07	43.13	67.71	79.43	110.76
Lodging on trips	341.61	81.37	126.48	189.82	243.26	424.07	450.83	964.61
Luggage	13.79	6.15	13.67	4.66	12.42	12.15	10.35	31.67
Parking fees and tolls on trips	11.22	2.59	4.60	6.08	11.63	14.45	17.00	27.27
Recreational expenses on trips	128.49	31.45	47.18	64.96	111.35	130.54	181.94	352.89
Restaurants and carry-outs on trips	257.15	64.47	103.30	157.93	206.50	312.12	382.96	669.19
Ship fares	56.53	4.90	21.78	33.72	28.15	20.43	69.73	193.60
Taxis and local transportation on trips	17.81	3.54	5.55	6.11	16.08	15.04	18.24	56.11
Train fares, intercity	18.88	10.32	7.41	14.44	13.89	15.72	13.81	51.59
Vehicle rental on trips	25.38	3.68	9.76	11.56	19.21	18.53	32.73	78.60

Source: Bureau of Labor Statistics, unpublished tables from the 2012 Consumer Expenditure Survey; calculations by New Strategist

Table 9. Travel: Indexed spending by income, 2012

(indexed average annual spending of consumer units on travel, by before-tax income of consumer unit, 2012; index definition: an index of 100 is the average for all consumer units; an index of 125 means that spending by consumer units in that group is 25 percent above the average for all consumer units; an index of 75 indicates spending that is 25 percent below the average for all consumer units)

	total consumer units	under $20,000	$20,000– $39,999	$40,000– $49,999	$50,000– $69,999	$70,000– $79,999	$80,000– $99,999	$100,000 or more
Average spending of consumer units, total	**$51,442**	**$22,405**	**$33,455**	**$41,567**	**$49,982**	**$59,984**	**$67,418**	**$101,423**
Average spending of consumer units, index	**100**	**44**	**65**	**81**	**97**	**117**	**131**	**197**
TRAVEL	**100**	**26**	**42**	**59**	**82**	**112**	**136**	**265**
Airline fares	100	27	40	55	87	103	121	275
Alcoholic beverages purchased on trips	100	24	32	62	84	97	157	271
Bus fares, intercity	100	53	59	58	108	115	144	192
Gasoline and motor oil on trips	100	33	63	80	102	142	164	185
Groceries on trips	100	31	56	66	86	135	158	221
Lodging on trips	100	24	37	56	71	124	132	282
Luggage	100	45	99	34	90	88	75	230
Parking fees and tolls on trips	100	23	41	54	104	129	152	243
Recreational expenses on trips	100	24	37	51	87	102	142	275
Restaurants and carry-outs on trips	100	25	40	61	80	121	149	260
Ship fares	100	9	39	60	50	36	123	342
Taxis and local transportation on trips	100	20	31	34	90	84	102	315
Train fares, intercity	100	55	39	76	74	83	73	273
Vehicle rental on trips	100	15	38	46	76	73	129	310

Source: Calculations by New Strategist based on the Bureau of Labor Statistics' 2012 Consumer Expenditure Survey

Table 10. Travel: Total spending by income, 2012

(total annual spending on travel, by before-tax income group of consumer units, 2012; consumer units and dollars in thousands)

	total consumer units	under $20,000	$20,000– $39,999	$40,000– $49,999	$50,000– $69,999	$70,000– $79,999	$80,000– $99,999	$100,000 or more
Number of consumer units	124,416	26,177	28,041	11,010	17,972	6,946	10,977	23,293
Total spending of all consumer units	$6,400,191,698	$586,484,559	$938,098,035	$457,656,413	$898,268,776	$416,649,836	$740,046,398	$2,362,436,389
TRAVEL	183,930,394	10,101,481	17,472,233	9,576,168	21,807,225	11,542,932	22,096,152	91,376,343
Airline fares	43,860,372	2,504,278	3,944,561	2,136,601	5,492,423	2,521,745	4,677,300	22,582,796
Alcoholic beverages purchased on trips	5,449,421	277,875	398,814	298,481	663,167	296,039	755,218	2,760,453
Bus fares, intercity	1,488,015	164,711	197,072	76,079	231,839	95,855	188,475	534,574
Gasoline and motor oil on trips	18,534,252	1,291,644	2,622,773	1,313,933	2,738,394	1,469,635	2,676,851	6,420,715
Groceries on trips	6,249,416	405,771	782,448	364,101	775,132	470,314	871,903	2,579,933
Lodging on trips	42,501,750	2,129,942	3,546,618	2,089,918	4,371,869	2,945,590	4,948,761	22,468,661
Luggage	1,715,697	161,059	383,307	51,307	223,212	84,394	113,612	737,689
Parking fees and tolls on trips	1,395,948	67,893	129,117	66,941	209,014	100,370	186,609	635,200
Recreational expenses on trips	15,986,212	823,164	1,322,933	715,210	2,001,182	906,731	1,997,155	8,219,867
Restaurants and carry-outs on trips	31,993,574	1,687,550	2,896,735	1,738,809	3,711,218	2,167,986	4,203,752	15,587,443
Ship fares	7,033,236	128,273	610,727	371,257	505,912	141,907	765,426	4,509,525
Taxis and local transportation on trips	2,215,849	92,772	155,717	67,271	288,990	104,468	200,220	1,306,970
Train fares, intercity	2,348,974	270,111	207,721	158,984	249,631	109,191	151,592	1,201,686
Vehicle rental on trips	3,157,678	96,438	273,689	127,276	345,242	128,709	359,277	1,830,830

Note: Numbers may not add to total because of rounding.
Source: Calculations by New Strategist based on the Bureau of Labor Statistics' 2012 Consumer Expenditure Survey

Table 11. Travel: Market shares by income, 2012

(percentage of total annual spending on travel accounted for by before-tax income group of consumer units, 2012)

	total consumer units	under $20,000	$20,000– $39,999	$40,000– $49,999	$50,000– $69,999	$70,000– $79,999	$80,000– $99,999	$100,000 or more
Share of total consumer units	**100.0%**	**21.0%**	**22.5%**	**8.8%**	**14.4%**	**5.6%**	**8.8%**	**18.7%**
Share of total before-tax income	**100.0**	**3.4**	**10.2**	**6.0**	**13.1**	**6.4**	**12.0**	**49.1**
Share of total spending	**100.0**	**9.2**	**14.7**	**7.2**	**14.0**	**6.5**	**11.6**	**36.9**
TRAVEL	**100.0**	**5.5**	**9.5**	**5.2**	**11.9**	**6.3**	**12.0**	**49.7**
Airline fares	100.0	5.7	9.0	4.9	12.5	5.7	10.7	51.5
Alcoholic beverages purchased on trips	100.0	5.1	7.3	5.5	12.2	5.4	13.9	50.7
Bus fares, intercity	100.0	11.1	13.2	5.1	15.6	6.4	12.7	35.9
Gasoline and motor oil on trips	100.0	7.0	14.2	7.1	14.8	7.9	14.4	34.6
Groceries on trips	100.0	6.5	12.5	5.8	12.4	7.5	14.0	41.3
Lodging on trips	100.0	5.0	8.3	4.9	10.3	6.9	11.6	52.9
Luggage	100.0	9.4	22.3	3.0	13.0	4.9	6.6	43.0
Parking fees and tolls on trips	100.0	4.9	9.2	4.8	15.0	7.2	13.4	45.5
Recreational expenses on trips	100.0	5.1	8.3	4.5	12.5	5.7	12.5	51.4
Restaurants and carry-outs on trips	100.0	5.3	9.1	5.4	11.6	6.8	13.1	48.7
Ship fares	100.0	1.8	8.7	5.3	7.2	2.0	10.9	64.1
Taxis and local transportation on trips	100.0	4.2	7.0	3.0	13.0	4.7	9.0	59.0
Train fares, intercity	100.0	11.5	8.8	6.8	10.6	4.6	6.5	51.2
Vehicle rental on trips	100.0	3.1	8.7	4.0	10.9	4.1	11.4	58.0

Note: Numbers may not add to total because of rounding.
Source: Calculations by New Strategist based on the Bureau of Labor Statistics' 2012 Consumer Expenditure Survey

Table 12. Travel: Average spending by high-income consumer units, 2012

(average annual spending on travel, by before-tax income of consumer units with high incomes, 2012)

	total consumer units	$100,000 or more	$100,000– $119,999	$120,000– $149,999	$150,000 or more
Number of consumer units (in 000s)	124,416	23,293	7,183	6,947	9,162
Number of persons per consumer unit	2.5	3.2	3.1	3.2	3.2
Average before-tax income of consumer units	$65,596.00	$171,910.00	$108,977.00	$132,318.00	$251,270.00
Average spending of consumer units, total	51,441.87	101,422.59	77,965.87	89,521.33	129,211.07
TRAVEL	1,478.35	3,922.91	2,518.17	3,354.06	5,457.65
Airline fares	352.53	969.51	543.87	828.55	1,410.10
Alcoholic beverages purchased on trips	43.80	118.51	84.74	88.97	167.37
Bus fares, intercity	11.96	22.95	15.92	18.08	32.14
Gasoline and motor oil on trips	148.97	275.65	256.90	270.53	294.22
Groceries on trips	50.23	110.76	87.04	94.86	141.40
Lodging on trips	341.61	964.61	615.91	841.85	1,331.09
Luggage	13.79	31.67	9.50	21.44	58.94
Parking fees and tolls on trips	11.22	27.27	19.51	22.91	36.67
Recreational expenses on trips	128.49	352.89	238.29	276.74	500.48
Restaurants and carry-outs on trips	257.15	669.19	446.91	606.11	891.29
Ship fares	56.53	193.60	102.01	120.11	321.14
Taxis and local transportation on trips	17.81	56.11	26.35	41.67	90.38
Train fares, intercity	18.88	51.59	27.98	41.56	77.69
Vehicle rental on trips	25.38	78.60	43.24	80.68	104.74

Source: Bureau of Labor Statistics, unpublished tables from the 2012 Consumer Expenditure Survey; calculations by New Strategist

Table 13. Travel: Indexed spending by high-income consumer units, 2012

(indexed average annual spending of consumer units with high incomes on travel, by before-tax income of consumer unit, 2012; index definition: an index of 100 is the average for all consumer units; an index of 125 means that spending by consumer units in that group is 25 percent above the average for all consumer units; an index of 75 indicates spending that is 25 percent below the average for all consumer units)

	total consumer units	$100,000 or more	$100,000– $119,999	$120,000– $149,999	$150,000 or more
Average spending of consumer units, total	**$51,442**	**$101,423**	**$77,966**	**$89,521**	**$129,211**
Average spending of consumer units, index	**100**	**197**	**152**	**174**	**251**
TRAVEL	**100**	**265**	**170**	**227**	**369**
Airline fares	100	275	154	235	400
Alcoholic beverages purchased on trips	100	271	193	203	382
Bus fares, intercity	100	192	133	151	269
Gasoline and motor oil on trips	100	185	172	182	198
Groceries on trips	100	221	173	189	282
Lodging on trips	100	282	180	246	390
Luggage	100	230	69	155	427
Parking fees and tolls on trips	100	243	174	204	327
Recreational expenses on trips	100	275	185	215	390
Restaurants and carry-outs on trips	100	260	174	236	347
Ship fares	100	342	180	212	568
Taxis and local transportation on trips	100	315	148	234	507
Train fares, intercity	100	273	148	220	411
Vehicle rental on trips	100	310	170	318	413

Source: Calculations by New Strategist based on the Bureau of Labor Statistics' 2012 Consumer Expenditure Survey

Table 14. Travel: Total spending by high-income consumer units, 2012

(total annual spending on travel, by before-tax income group of consumer units with high incomes, 2012; consumer units and dollars in thousands)

	total consumer units	$100,000 or more	$100,000–$119,999	$120,000–$149,999	$150,000 or more
Number of consumer units	124,416	23,293	7,183	6,947	9,162
Total spending of all consumer units	$6,400,191,698	$2,362,436,389	$560,028,844	$621,904,680	$1,183,831,823
TRAVEL	**183,930,394**	**91,376,343**	**18,088,015**	**23,300,655**	**50,002,989**
Airline fares	43,860,372	22,582,796	3,906,618	5,755,937	12,919,336
Alcoholic beverages purchased on trips	5,449,421	2,760,453	608,687	618,075	1,533,444
Bus fares, intercity	1,488,015	534,574	114,353	125,602	294,467
Gasoline and motor oil on trips	18,534,252	6,420,715	1,845,313	1,879,372	2,695,644
Groceries on trips	6,249,416	2,579,933	625,208	658,992	1,295,507
Lodging on trips	42,501,750	22,468,661	4,424,082	5,848,332	12,195,447
Luggage	1,715,697	737,689	68,239	148,944	540,008
Parking fees and tolls on trips	1,395,948	635,200	140,140	159,156	335,971
Recreational expenses on trips	15,986,212	8,219,867	1,711,637	1,922,513	4,585,398
Restaurants and carry-outs on trips	31,993,574	15,587,443	3,210,155	4,210,646	8,165,999
Ship fares	7,033,236	4,509,525	732,738	834,404	2,942,285
Taxis and local transportation on trips	2,215,849	1,306,970	189,272	289,481	828,062
Train fares, intercity	2,348,974	1,201,686	200,980	288,717	711,796
Vehicle rental on trips	3,157,678	1,830,830	310,593	560,484	959,628

Note: Numbers may not add to total because of rounding.
Source: Calculations by New Strategist based on the Bureau of Labor Statistics' 2012 Consumer Expenditure Survey

Table 15. Travel: Market shares by high-income consumer units, 2012

(percentage of total annual spending on travel accounted for by before-tax income group of consumer units with high incomes, 2012)

	total consumer units	$100,000 or more	$100,000– $119,999	$120,000– $149,999	$150,000 or more
Share of total consumer units	100.0%	18.7%	5.8%	5.6%	7.4%
Share of total before-tax income	100.0	49.1	9.6	11.3	28.2
Share of total spending	100.0	36.9	8.8	9.7	18.5
TRAVEL	100.0	49.7	9.8	12.7	27.2
Airline fares	100.0	51.5	8.9	13.1	29.5
Alcoholic beverages purchased on trips	100.0	50.7	11.2	11.3	28.1
Bus fares, intercity	100.0	35.9	7.7	8.4	19.8
Gasoline and motor oil on trips	100.0	34.6	10.0	10.1	14.5
Groceries on trips	100.0	41.3	10.0	10.5	20.7
Lodging on trips	100.0	52.9	10.4	13.8	28.7
Luggage	100.0	43.0	4.0	8.7	31.5
Parking fees and tolls on trips	100.0	45.5	10.0	11.4	24.1
Recreational expenses on trips	100.0	51.4	10.7	12.0	28.7
Restaurants and carry-outs on trips	100.0	48.7	10.0	13.2	25.5
Ship fares	100.0	64.1	10.4	11.9	41.8
Taxis and local transportation on trips	100.0	59.0	8.5	13.1	37.4
Train fares, intercity	100.0	51.2	8.6	12.3	30.3
Vehicle rental on trips	100.0	58.0	9.8	17.7	30.4

Note: Numbers may not add to total because of rounding.
Source: Calculations by New Strategist based on the Bureau of Labor Statistics' 2012 Consumer Expenditure Survey

Table 16. Travel: Average spending by household type, 2012

(average annual spending of consumer units on travel, by type of consumer unit, 2012)

	total consumer units	total married couples	married couples, no children	married couples with children				single parent with child under age 18	single person
				total	oldest child under age 6	oldest child aged 6 to 17	oldest child aged 18 or older		
Number of consumer units (in 000s)	124,416	60,428	25,936	29,252	5,676	14,797	8,778	6,524	36,942
Number of persons per consumer unit	2.5	3.2	2.0	3.9	3.5	4.2	3.9	2.9	1.0
Average before-tax income of consumer units	$65,596.00	$90,393.00	$81,717.00	$98,104.00	$85,200.00	$100,698.00	$102,074.00	$34,194.00	$34,102.00
Average spending of consumer units, total	51,441.87	67,310.04	61,284.60	72,814.06	64,103.17	74,658.88	75,286.36	38,667.27	30,715.83
TRAVEL	**1,478.35**	**2,196.49**	**2,500.24**	**2,070.05**	**1,538.85**	**2,273.16**	**2,071.29**	**624.01**	**781.72**
Airline fares	352.53	510.99	540.00	510.34	390.95	534.99	546.01	132.19	208.54
Alcoholic beverages purchased on trips	43.80	59.60	77.66	48.43	49.77	49.47	45.79	14.50	29.67
Bus fares, intercity	11.96	16.30	20.13	12.83	9.04	11.38	17.73	4.74	7.92
Gasoline and motor oil on trips	148.97	219.03	248.26	204.32	191.67	218.48	188.62	73.56	74.07
Groceries on trips	50.23	74.10	89.21	66.03	45.26	77.90	59.45	26.05	23.77
Lodging on trips	341.61	523.87	609.63	481.03	327.60	534.01	490.94	138.18	161.26
Luggage	13.79	18.40	18.51	21.03	18.46	27.54	11.77	14.67	6.78
Parking fees and tolls on trips	11.22	16.13	17.59	15.16	14.08	17.38	12.12	5.79	5.81
Recreational expenses on trips	128.49	195.23	200.57	209.27	116.10	266.00	173.90	57.12	66.59
Restaurants and carry-outs on trips	257.15	381.63	439.38	358.93	267.92	390.44	364.67	114.33	135.77
Ship fares	56.53	92.07	127.16	68.10	46.73	70.64	77.64	16.40	21.64
Taxis and local transportation on trips	17.81	25.51	30.83	22.71	21.00	19.53	29.19	7.89	11.52
Train fares, intercity	18.88	26.19	36.99	18.20	15.11	18.59	19.55	7.97	15.54
Vehicle rental on trips	25.38	37.44	44.32	33.67	25.16	36.81	33.91	10.62	12.84

Source: Bureau of Labor Statistics, unpublished data from the 2012 Consumer Expenditure Survey; calculations by New Strategist

Table 17. Travel: Indexed spending by household type, 2012

(indexed average annual spending of consumer units on travel, by type of consumer unit, 2012; index definition: an index of 100 is the average for all consumer units; an index of 125 means that spending by consumer units in that group is 25 percent above the average for all consumer units; an index of 75 indicates spending that is 25 percent below the average for all consumer units)

	total consumer units	total married couples	married couples, no children	married couples with children				single parent with child under age 18	single person
				total	oldest child under age 6	oldest child aged 6 to 17	oldest child aged 18 or older		
Average spending of consumer units, total	$51,442	$67,310	$61,285	$72,814	$64,103	$74,659	$75,286	$38,667	$30,716
Average spending of consumer units, index	100	131	119	142	125	145	146	75	60
TRAVEL	**100**	**149**	**169**	**140**	**104**	**154**	**140**	**42**	**53**
Airline fares	100	145	153	145	111	152	155	37	59
Alcoholic beverages purchased on trips	100	136	177	111	114	113	105	33	68
Bus fares, intercity	100	136	168	107	76	95	148	40	66
Gasoline and motor oil on trips	100	147	167	137	129	147	127	49	50
Groceries on trips	100	148	178	131	90	155	118	52	47
Lodging on trips	100	153	178	141	96	156	144	40	47
Luggage	100	133	134	153	134	200	85	106	49
Parking fees and tolls on trips	100	144	157	135	125	155	108	52	52
Recreational expenses on trips	100	152	156	163	90	207	135	44	52
Restaurants and carry-outs on trips	100	148	171	140	104	152	142	44	53
Ship fares	100	163	225	120	83	125	137	29	38
Taxis and local transportation on trips	100	143	173	128	118	110	164	44	65
Train fares, intercity	100	139	196	96	80	98	104	42	82
Vehicle rental on trips	100	148	175	133	99	145	134	42	51

Source: Calculations by New Strategist based on the Bureau of Labor Statistics' 2012 Consumer Expenditure Survey

Table 18. Travel: Total spending by household type, 2012

(total annual spending on travel, by consumer unit type, 2012; consumer units and dollars in thousands)

| | total consumer units | total married couples | married couples, no children | married couples with children | | | | single parent with child under age 18 | single person |
				total	oldest child under age 6	oldest child aged 6 to 17	oldest child aged 18 or older		
Number of consumer units	124,416	60,428	25,936	29,252	5,676	14,797	8,778	6,524	36,942
Total spending of all consumer units	$6,400,191,698	$4,067,411,097	$1,589,477,386	$2,129,956,883	$363,849,593	$1,104,727,447	$660,863,668	$252,265,269	$1,134,704,192
TRAVEL	183,930,394	132,729,498	64,846,225	60,553,103	8,734,513	33,635,949	18,181,784	4,071,041	28,878,300
Airline fares	43,860,372	30,878,104	14,005,440	14,928,466	2,219,032	7,916,247	4,792,876	862,408	7,703,885
Alcoholic beverages purchased on trips	5,449,421	3,601,509	2,014,190	1,416,674	282,495	732,008	401,945	94,598	1,096,069
Bus fares, intercity	1,488,015	984,976	522,092	375,303	51,311	168,390	155,634	30,924	292,581
Gasoline and motor oil on trips	18,534,252	13,235,545	6,438,871	5,976,769	1,087,919	3,232,849	1,655,706	479,905	2,736,294
Groceries on trips	6,249,416	4,477,715	2,313,751	1,931,510	256,896	1,152,686	521,852	169,950	878,111
Lodging on trips	42,501,750	31,656,416	15,811,364	14,071,090	1,859,458	7,901,746	4,309,471	901,486	5,957,267
Luggage	1,715,697	1,111,875	480,075	615,170	104,779	407,509	103,317	95,707	250,467
Parking fees and tolls on trips	1,395,948	974,704	456,214	443,460	79,918	257,172	106,389	37,774	214,633
Recreational expenses on trips	15,986,212	11,797,358	5,201,984	6,121,566	658,984	3,936,002	1,526,494	372,651	2,459,968
Restaurants and carry-outs on trips	31,993,574	23,061,138	11,395,760	10,499,420	1,520,714	5,777,341	3,201,073	745,889	5,015,615
Ship fares	7,033,236	5,563,606	3,298,022	1,992,061	265,239	1,045,260	681,524	106,994	799,425
Taxis and local transportation on trips	2,215,849	1,541,518	799,607	664,313	119,196	288,985	256,230	51,474	425,572
Train fares, intercity	2,348,974	1,582,609	959,373	532,386	85,764	275,076	171,610	51,996	574,079
Vehicle rental on trips	3,157,678	2,262,424	1,149,484	984,915	142,808	544,678	297,662	69,285	474,335

Note: Numbers do not add to total because not all types of consumer units are shown and because of rounding.
Source: Calculations by New Strategist based on the Bureau of Labor Statistics' 2012 Consumer Expenditure Survey

Table 19. Travel: Market shares by household type, 2012

(percentage of total annual spending on travel accounted for by types of consumer units, 2012)

	total consumer units	total married couples	married couples, no children	married couples with children				single parent with child under age 18	single person
				total	oldest child under age 6	oldest child aged 6 to 17	oldest child aged 18 or older		
Share of total consumer units	**100.0%**	**48.6%**	**20.8%**	**23.5%**	**4.6%**	**11.9%**	**7.1%**	**5.2%**	**29.7%**
Share of total before-tax income	**100.0**	**66.9**	**26.0**	**35.2**	**5.9**	**18.3**	**11.0**	**2.7**	**15.4**
Share of total spending	**100.0**	**63.6**	**24.8**	**33.3**	**5.7**	**17.3**	**10.3**	**3.9**	**17.7**
TRAVEL	**100.0**	**72.2**	**35.3**	**32.9**	**4.7**	**18.3**	**9.9**	**2.2**	**15.7**
Airline fares	100.0	70.4	31.9	34.0	5.1	18.0	10.9	2.0	17.6
Alcoholic beverages purchased on trips	100.0	66.1	37.0	26.0	5.2	13.4	7.4	1.7	20.1
Bus fares, intercity	100.0	66.2	35.1	25.2	3.4	11.3	10.5	2.1	19.7
Gasoline and motor oil on trips	100.0	71.4	34.7	32.2	5.9	17.4	8.9	2.6	14.8
Groceries on trips	100.0	71.7	37.0	30.9	4.1	18.4	8.4	2.7	14.1
Lodging on trips	100.0	74.5	37.2	33.1	4.4	18.6	10.1	2.1	14.0
Luggage	100.0	64.8	28.0	35.9	6.1	23.8	6.0	5.6	14.6
Parking fees and tolls on trips	100.0	69.8	32.7	31.8	5.7	18.4	7.6	2.7	15.4
Recreational expenses on trips	100.0	73.8	32.5	38.3	4.1	24.6	9.5	2.3	15.4
Restaurants and carry-outs on trips	100.0	72.1	35.6	32.8	4.8	18.1	10.0	2.3	15.7
Ship fares	100.0	79.1	46.9	28.3	3.8	14.9	9.7	1.5	11.4
Taxis and local transportation on trips	100.0	69.6	36.1	30.0	5.4	13.0	11.6	2.3	19.2
Train fares, intercity	100.0	67.4	40.8	22.7	3.7	11.7	7.3	2.2	24.4
Vehicle rental on trips	100.0	71.6	36.4	31.2	4.5	17.2	9.4	2.2	15.0

Note: Market shares by type of consumer unit do not add to total because not all types of consumer units are shown.
Source: Calculations by New Strategist based on the Bureau of Labor Statistics' 2012 Consumer Expenditure Survey

Table 20. Travel: Average spending by race and Hispanic origin, 2012

(average annual spending of consumer units on travel, by race and Hispanic origin of consumer unit reference person, 2012)

	total consumer units	Asian	black	Hispanic	non-Hispanic white and other
Number of consumer units (in 000s)	124,416	5,393	15,637	15,597	93,385
Number of persons per consumer unit	2.5	2.8	2.5	3.3	2.3
Average before-tax income of consumer units	$65,596.00	$86,156.00	$47,119.00	$48,066.00	$71,552.00
Average spending of consumer units, total	51,441.87	61,399.02	38,626.84	42,267.55	55,096.53
TRAVEL	**1,478.35**	**2,426.83**	**627.65**	**731.77**	**1,743.33**
Airline fares	352.53	986.90	150.78	217.24	408.38
Alcoholic beverages purchased on trips	43.80	37.59	14.51	21.94	52.29
Bus fares, intercity	11.96	23.87	8.73	11.51	12.60
Gasoline and motor oil on trips	148.97	111.56	73.29	91.51	171.03
Groceries on trips	50.23	53.06	18.58	28.60	59.08
Lodging on trips	341.61	397.20	142.16	114.68	412.30
Luggage	13.79	9.90	6.61	4.90	16.45
Parking fees and tolls on trips	11.22	14.68	5.06	8.05	12.78
Recreational expenses on trips	128.49	182.80	43.78	52.79	155.17
Restaurants and carry-outs on trips	257.15	384.23	106.44	132.11	302.84
Ship fares	56.53	119.70	22.08	23.53	67.81
Taxis and local transportation on trips	17.81	36.27	9.38	9.89	20.53
Train fares, intercity	18.88	33.30	8.31	7.40	22.54
Vehicle rental on trips	25.38	35.77	17.94	7.62	29.53

Note: "Asian" and "black" include Hispanics and non-Hispanics who identify themselves as being of the respective race alone. "Hispanic" includes people of any race who identify themselves as Hispanic. "Other" includes people who identify themselves as non-Hispanic and as Alaska Native, American Indian, Asian (who are also included in the "Asian" column), Native Hawaiian or other Pacific Islander, as well as non-Hispanics reporting more than one race.
Source: Bureau of Labor Statistics, unpublished tables from the 2012 Consumer Expenditure Survey; calculations by New Strategist

Table 21. Travel: Indexed spending by race and Hispanic origin, 2012

(indexed average annual spending of consumer units on travel, by race and Hispanic origin of consumer unit reference person, 2012; index definition: an index of 100 is the average for all consumer units; an index of 125 means that spending by consumer units in that group is 25 percent above the average for all consumer units; an index of 75 indicates spending that is 25 percent below the average for all consumer units)

	total consumer units	Asian	black	Hispanic	non-Hispanic white and other
Average spending of consumer units, total	**$51,442**	**$61,399**	**$38,627**	**$42,268**	**$55,097**
Average spending of consumer units, index	**100**	**119**	**75**	**82**	**107**
TRAVEL	**100**	**164**	**42**	**49**	**118**
Airline fares	100	280	43	62	116
Alcoholic beverages purchased on trips	100	86	33	50	119
Bus fares, intercity	100	200	73	96	105
Gasoline and motor oil on trips	100	75	49	61	115
Groceries on trips	100	106	37	57	118
Lodging on trips	100	116	42	34	121
Luggage	100	72	48	36	119
Parking fees and tolls on trips	100	131	45	72	114
Recreational expenses on trips	100	142	34	41	121
Restaurants and carry-outs on trips	100	149	41	51	118
Ship fares	100	212	39	42	120
Taxis and local transportation on trips	100	204	53	56	115
Train fares, intercity	100	176	44	39	119
Vehicle rental on trips	100	141	71	30	116

Note: "Asian" and "black" include Hispanics and non-Hispanics who identify themselves as being of the respective race alone. "Hispanic" includes people of any race who identify themselves as Hispanic. "Other" includes people who identify themselves as non-Hispanic and as Alaska Native, American Indian, Asian (who are also included in the "Asian" column), Native Hawaiian or other Pacific Islander, as well as non-Hispanics reporting more than one race.
Source: Calculations by New Strategist based on the Bureau of Labor Statistics' 2012 Consumer Expenditure Survey

Table 22. Travel: Total spending by race and Hispanic origin, 2012

(total annual spending on travel, by consumer unit race and Hispanic origin groups, 2012; consumer units and dollars in thousands)

	total consumer units	Asian	black	Hispanic	non-Hispanic white and other
Number of consumer units	**124,416**	**5,393**	**15,637**	**15,597**	**93,385**
Total spending of all consumer units	**$6,400,191,698**	**$331,124,915**	**$604,007,897**	**$659,246,977**	**$5,145,189,454**
TRAVEL	**183,930,394**	**13,087,894**	**9,814,563**	**11,413,417**	**162,800,872**
Airline fares	43,860,372	5,322,352	2,357,747	3,388,292	38,136,566
Alcoholic beverages purchased on trips	5,449,421	202,723	226,893	342,198	4,883,102
Bus fares, intercity	1,488,015	128,731	136,511	179,521	1,176,651
Gasoline and motor oil on trips	18,534,252	601,643	1,146,036	1,427,281	15,971,637
Groceries on trips	6,249,416	286,153	290,535	446,074	5,317,186
Lodging on trips	42,501,750	2,142,100	2,222,956	1,788,664	38,502,636
Luggage	1,715,697	53,391	103,361	76,425	1,536,183
Parking fees and tolls on trips	1,395,948	79,169	79,123	125,556	1,193,460
Recreational expenses on trips	15,986,212	985,840	684,588	823,366	14,490,550
Restaurants and carry-outs on trips	31,993,574	2,072,152	1,664,402	2,060,520	28,280,713
Ship fares	7,033,236	645,542	345,265	366,997	6,332,437
Taxis and local transportation on trips	2,215,849	195,604	146,675	154,254	1,917,194
Train fares, intercity	2,348,974	179,587	129,943	115,418	2,104,898
Vehicle rental on trips	3,157,678	192,908	280,528	118,849	2,757,659

Note: "Asian" and "black" include Hispanics and non-Hispanics who identify themselves as being of the respective race alone. "Hispanic" includes people of any race who identify themselves as Hispanic. "Other" includes people who identify themselves as non-Hispanic and as Alaska Native, American Indian, Asian (who are also included in the "Asian" column), Native Hawaiian or other Pacific Islander, as well as non-Hispanics reporting more than one race. Numbers may not add to total because of rounding.
Source: Calculations by New Strategist based on the Bureau of Labor Statistics' 2012 Consumer Expenditure Survey

Table 23. Travel: Market shares by race and Hispanic origin, 2012

(percentage of total annual spending on travel accounted for by consumer unit race and Hispanic origin groups, 2012)

	total consumer units	Asian	black	Hispanic	non-Hispanic white and other
Share of total consumer units	100.0%	4.3%	12.6%	12.5%	75.1%
Share of total before-tax income	100.0	5.7	9.0	9.2	81.9
Share of total spending	100.0	5.2	9.4	10.3	80.4
TRAVEL	100.0	7.1	5.3	6.2	88.5
Airline fares	100.0	12.1	5.4	7.7	86.9
Alcoholic beverages purchased on trips	100.0	3.7	4.2	6.3	89.6
Bus fares, intercity	100.0	8.7	9.2	12.1	79.1
Gasoline and motor oil on trips	100.0	3.2	6.2	7.7	86.2
Groceries on trips	100.0	4.6	4.6	7.1	88.3
Lodging on trips	100.0	5.0	5.2	4.2	90.6
Luggage	100.0	3.1	6.0	4.5	89.5
Parking fees and tolls on trips	100.0	5.7	5.7	9.0	85.5
Recreational expenses on trips	100.0	6.2	4.3	5.2	90.6
Restaurants and carry-outs on trips	100.0	6.5	5.2	6.4	88.4
Ship fares	100.0	9.2	4.9	5.2	90.0
Taxis and local transportation on trips	100.0	8.8	6.6	7.0	86.5
Train fares, intercity	100.0	7.6	5.5	4.9	89.6
Vehicle rental on trips	100.0	6.1	8.9	3.8	87.3

Note: "Asian" and "black" include Hispanics and non-Hispanics who identify themselves as being of the respective race alone. "Hispanic" includes people of any race who identify themselves as Hispanic. "Other" includes people who identify themselves as non-Hispanic and as Alaska Native, American Indian, Asian (who are also included in the "Asian" column), Native Hawaiian or other Pacific Islander, as well as non-Hispanics reporting more than one race.
Source: Calculations by New Strategist based on the Bureau of Labor Statistics' 2012 Consumer Expenditure Survey

Table 24. Travel: Average spending by region, 2012

(average annual spending of consumer units on travel, by region in which consumer unit lives, 2012)

	total consumer units	Northeast	Midwest	South	West
Number of consumer units (in 000s)	**124,416**	**22,459**	**27,584**	**46,338**	**28,035**
Number of persons per consumer unit	**2.5**	**2.4**	**2.4**	**2.5**	**2.6**
Average before-tax income of consumer units	**$65,596.00**	**$72,036.00**	**$65,217.00**	**$60,219.00**	**$69,700.00**
Average spending of consumer units, total	**51,441.87**	**55,883.88**	**48,602.08**	**47,756.69**	**56,782.20**
TRAVEL	**1,478.35**	**1,651.74**	**1,377.04**	**1,233.67**	**1,843.58**
Airline fares	352.53	447.89	304.40	253.02	487.96
Alcoholic beverages purchased on trips	43.80	47.75	44.25	36.64	52.05
Bus fares, intercity	11.96	13.94	11.13	10.57	13.52
Gasoline and motor oil on trips	148.97	107.03	169.99	141.98	173.43
Groceries on trips	50.23	50.20	44.88	44.01	65.81
Lodging on trips	341.61	381.23	328.23	294.30	401.22
Luggage	13.79	15.14	13.29	13.51	13.67
Parking fees and tolls on trips	11.22	17.48	10.48	8.85	10.84
Recreational expenses on trips	128.49	139.47	115.25	106.51	169.06
Restaurants and carry-outs on trips	257.15	273.45	240.97	227.86	308.42
Ship fares	56.53	87.16	37.10	45.02	70.14
Taxis and local transportation on trips	17.81	26.01	15.03	13.54	21.03
Train fares, intercity	18.88	21.95	19.01	14.10	24.19
Vehicle rental on trips	25.38	23.04	23.03	23.76	32.24

Source: Bureau of Labor Statistics, unpublished data from the 2012 Consumer Expenditure Survey; calculations by New Strategist

Table 25. Travel: Indexed spending by region, 2012

(indexed average annual spending of consumer units on travel, by region in which consumer unit lives, 2012; index definition: an index of 100 is the average for all consumer units; an index of 125 means that spending by consumer units in that group is 25 percent above the average for all consumer units; an index of 75 indicates spending that is 25 percent below the average for all consumer units)

	total consumer units	Northeast	Midwest	South	West
Average spending of consumer units, total	**$51,442**	**$55,884**	**$48,602**	**$47,757**	**$56,782**
Average spending of consumer units, index	**100**	**109**	**94**	**93**	**110**
TRAVEL	**100**	**112**	**93**	**83**	**125**
Airline fares	100	127	86	72	138
Alcoholic beverages purchased on trips	100	109	101	84	119
Bus fares, intercity	100	117	93	88	113
Gasoline and motor oil on trips	100	72	114	95	116
Groceries on trips	100	100	89	88	131
Lodging on trips	100	112	96	86	117
Luggage	100	110	96	98	99
Parking fees and tolls on trips	100	156	93	79	97
Recreational expenses on trips	100	109	90	83	132
Restaurants and carry-outs on trips	100	106	94	89	120
Ship fares	100	154	66	80	124
Taxis and local transportation on trips	100	146	84	76	118
Train fares, intercity	100	116	101	75	128
Vehicle rental on trips	100	91	91	94	127

Source: Calculations by New Strategist based on the Bureau of Labor Statistics' 2012 Consumer Expenditure Survey

Table 26. Travel: Total spending by region, 2012

(total annual spending on travel, by region in which consumer unit lives, 2012; consumer units and dollars in thousands)

	total consumer units	Northeast	Midwest	South	West
Number of consumer units	124,416	22,459	27,584	46,338	28,035
Total spending of all consumer units	$6,400,191,698	$1,255,096,061	$1,340,639,775	$2,212,949,501	$1,591,888,977
TRAVEL	183,930,394	37,096,429	37,984,271	57,165,800	51,684,765
Airline fares	43,860,372	10,059,162	8,396,570	11,724,441	13,679,959
Alcoholic beverages purchased on trips	5,449,421	1,072,417	1,220,592	1,697,824	1,459,222
Bus fares, intercity	1,488,015	313,078	307,010	489,793	379,033
Gasoline and motor oil on trips	18,534,252	2,403,787	4,689,004	6,579,069	4,862,110
Groceries on trips	6,249,416	1,127,442	1,237,970	2,039,335	1,844,983
Lodging on trips	42,501,750	8,562,045	9,053,896	13,637,273	11,248,203
Luggage	1,715,697	340,029	366,591	626,026	383,238
Parking fees and tolls on trips	1,395,948	392,583	289,080	410,091	303,899
Recreational expenses on trips	15,986,212	3,132,357	3,179,056	4,935,460	4,739,597
Restaurants and carry-outs on trips	31,993,574	6,141,414	6,646,916	10,558,577	8,646,555
Ship fares	7,033,236	1,957,526	1,023,366	2,086,137	1,966,375
Taxis and local transportation on trips	2,215,849	584,159	414,588	627,417	589,576
Train fares, intercity	2,348,974	492,975	524,372	653,366	678,167
Vehicle rental on trips	3,157,678	517,455	635,260	1,100,991	903,848

Note: Numbers may not add to total because of rounding.
Source: Calculations by New Strategist based on the Bureau of Labor Statistics' 2012 Consumer Expenditure Survey

Table 27. Travel: Market shares by region, 2012

(percentage of total annual spending on travel accounted for by consumer units by region of residence, 2012)

	total consumer units	Northeast	Midwest	South	West
Share of total consumer units	**100.0%**	**18.1%**	**22.2%**	**37.2%**	**22.5%**
Share of total before-tax income	**100.0**	**19.8**	**22.0**	**34.2**	**23.9**
Share of total spending	**100.0**	**19.6**	**20.9**	**34.6**	**24.9**
TRAVEL	**100.0**	**20.2**	**20.7**	**31.1**	**28.1**
Airline fares	100.0	22.9	19.1	26.7	31.2
Alcoholic beverages purchased on trips	100.0	19.7	22.4	31.2	26.8
Bus fares, intercity	100.0	21.0	20.6	32.9	25.5
Gasoline and motor oil on trips	100.0	13.0	25.3	35.5	26.2
Groceries on trips	100.0	18.0	19.8	32.6	29.5
Lodging on trips	100.0	20.1	21.3	32.1	26.5
Luggage	100.0	19.8	21.4	36.5	22.3
Parking fees and tolls on trips	100.0	28.1	20.7	29.4	21.8
Recreational expenses on trips	100.0	19.6	19.9	30.9	29.6
Restaurants and carry-outs on trips	100.0	19.2	20.8	33.0	27.0
Ship fares	100.0	27.8	14.6	29.7	28.0
Taxis and local transportation on trips	100.0	26.4	18.7	28.3	26.6
Train fares, intercity	100.0	21.0	22.3	27.8	28.9
Vehicle rental on trips	100.0	16.4	20.1	34.9	28.6

Note: Numbers may not add to total because of rounding.
Source: Calculations by New Strategist based on the Bureau of Labor Statistics' 2012 Consumer Expenditure Survey

Table 28. Travel: Average spending by education, 2012

(average annual spending of consumer units on travel, by education of consumer unit reference person, 2012)

	total consumer units	less than high school graduate	high school graduate	some college	associate's degree	bachelor's degree or more		
						total	bachelor's degree	master's, professional, doctorate
Number of consumer units (in 000s)	124,416	16,246	31,022	25,623	12,287	39,238	24,798	14,440
Number of persons per consumer unit	2.5	2.7	2.5	2.4	2.6	2.4	2.4	2.5
Average before-tax income of consumer units	$65,596.00	$33,154.00	$47,221.00	$55,987.00	$66,122.00	$99,667.00	$89,438.00	$117,233.00
Average spending of consumer units, total	51,441.87	31,193.61	39,989.36	46,118.38	52,414.41	71,926.33	66,420.24	81,363.01
TRAVEL	1,478.35	373.72	724.28	1,052.90	1,272.47	2,873.87	2,488.22	3,536.22
Airline fares	352.53	89.61	145.50	238.86	221.63	740.27	628.98	931.39
Alcoholic beverages purchased on trips	43.80	8.20	17.72	35.62	32.09	88.17	80.37	101.58
Bus fares, intercity	11.96	9.90	6.62	9.25	9.06	19.73	16.89	24.61
Gasoline and motor oil on trips	148.97	56.09	92.48	139.28	171.42	231.37	222.88	245.96
Groceries on trips	50.23	17.76	26.69	45.50	51.76	84.90	72.82	105.63
Lodging on trips	341.61	61.66	161.62	218.36	310.87	689.92	572.12	892.23
Luggage	13.79	5.58	13.02	10.64	12.16	20.10	21.26	18.15
Parking fees and tolls on trips	11.22	2.51	5.62	7.33	13.17	21.17	18.56	25.64
Recreational expenses on trips	128.49	31.80	64.22	89.74	119.43	247.48	228.64	279.85
Restaurants and carry-outs on trips	257.15	58.94	135.57	186.36	230.79	489.81	427.45	596.90
Ship fares	56.53	23.46	30.25	31.04	58.06	107.16	91.14	134.67
Taxis and local transportation on trips	17.81	4.13	6.78	10.41	11.85	38.90	34.59	46.32
Train fares, intercity	18.88	1.72	7.24	11.42	10.71	42.62	30.59	63.27
Vehicle rental on trips	25.38	2.36	10.95	19.09	19.47	52.27	41.93	70.02

Source: Bureau of Labor Statistics, unpublished data from the 2012 Consumer Expenditure Survey; calculations by New Strategist

Table 29. Travel: Indexed spending by education, 2012

(indexed average annual spending of consumer units on travel by education of consumer unit reference person, 2012; index definition: an index of 100 is the average for all consumer units; an index of 125 means that spending by consumer units in that group is 25 percent above the average for all consumer units; an index of 75 indicates spending that is 25 percent below the average for all consumer units)

	total consumer units	less than high school graduate	high school graduate	some college	associate's degree	bachelor's degree or more		
						total	bachelor's degree	master's, professional, doctorate
Average spending of consumer units, total	**$51,442**	**$31,194**	**$39,989**	**$46,118**	**$52,414**	**$71,926**	**$66,420**	**$81,363**
Average spending of consumer units, index	**100**	**61**	**78**	**90**	**102**	**140**	**129**	**158**
TRAVEL	**100**	**25**	**49**	**71**	**86**	**194**	**168**	**239**
Airline fares	100	25	41	68	63	210	178	264
Alcoholic beverages purchased on trips	100	19	40	81	73	201	183	232
Bus fares, intercity	100	83	55	77	76	165	141	206
Gasoline and motor oil on trips	100	38	62	93	115	155	150	165
Groceries on trips	100	35	53	91	103	169	145	210
Lodging on trips	100	18	47	64	91	202	167	261
Luggage	100	40	94	77	88	146	154	132
Parking fees and tolls on trips	100	22	50	65	117	189	165	229
Recreational expenses on trips	100	25	50	70	93	193	178	218
Restaurants and carry-outs on trips	100	23	53	72	90	190	166	232
Ship fares	100	42	54	55	103	190	161	238
Taxis and local transportation on trips	100	23	38	58	67	218	194	260
Train fares, intercity	100	9	38	60	57	226	162	335
Vehicle rental on trips	100	9	43	75	77	206	165	276

Source: Calculations by New Strategist based on the Bureau of Labor Statistics' 2012 Consumer Expenditure Survey

Table 30. Travel: Total spending by education, 2012

(total annual spending on travel, by consumer unit educational attainment group, 2012; consumer units and dollars in thousands)

	total consumer units	less than high school graduate	high school graduate	some college	associate's degree	bachelor's degree or more total	bachelor's degree	master's, professional, doctorate
Number of consumer units	124,416	16,246	31,022	25,623	12,287	39,238	24,798	14,440
Total spending of all consumer units	$6,400,191,698	$506,771,388	$1,240,549,926	$1,181,691,251	$644,015,856	$2,822,245,337	$1,647,089,112	$1,174,881,864
TRAVEL	**183,930,394**	**6,071,455**	**22,468,614**	**26,978,457**	**15,634,839**	**112,764,911**	**61,702,880**	**51,063,017**
Airline fares	43,860,372	1,455,804	4,513,701	6,120,310	2,723,168	29,046,714	15,597,446	13,449,272
Alcoholic beverages purchased on trips	5,449,421	133,217	549,710	912,691	394,290	3,459,614	1,993,015	1,466,815
Bus fares, intercity	1,488,015	160,835	205,366	237,013	111,320	774,166	418,838	355,368
Gasoline and motor oil on trips	18,534,252	911,238	2,868,915	3,568,771	2,106,238	9,078,496	5,526,978	3,551,662
Groceries on trips	6,249,416	288,529	827,977	1,165,847	635,975	3,331,306	1,805,790	1,525,297
Lodging on trips	42,501,750	1,001,728	5,013,776	5,595,038	3,819,660	27,071,081	14,187,432	12,883,801
Luggage	1,715,697	90,653	403,906	272,629	149,410	788,684	527,205	262,086
Parking fees and tolls on trips	1,395,948	40,777	174,344	187,817	161,820	830,668	460,251	370,242
Recreational expenses on trips	15,986,212	516,623	1,992,233	2,299,408	1,467,436	9,710,620	5,669,815	4,041,034
Restaurants and carry-outs on trips	31,993,574	957,539	4,205,653	4,775,102	2,835,717	19,219,165	10,599,905	8,619,236
Ship fares	7,033,236	381,131	938,416	795,338	713,383	4,204,744	2,260,090	1,944,635
Taxis and local transportation on trips	2,215,849	67,096	210,329	266,735	145,601	1,526,358	857,763	668,861
Train fares, intercity	2,348,974	27,943	224,599	292,615	131,594	1,672,324	758,571	913,619
Vehicle rental on trips	3,157,678	38,341	339,691	489,143	239,228	2,050,970	1,039,780	1,011,089

Note: Numbers may not add to total because of rounding.
Source: Calculations by New Strategist based on the Bureau of Labor Statistics' 2012 Consumer Expenditure Survey

Table 31. Travel: Market shares by education, 2012

(percentage of total annual spending on travel accounted for by consumer unit educational attainment groups, 2012)

	total consumer units	less than high school graduate	high school graduate	some college	associate's degree	bachelor's degree or more total	bachelor's degree	master's, professional, doctorate
Share of total consumer units	100.0%	13.1%	24.9%	20.6%	9.9%	31.5%	19.9%	11.6%
Share of total before-tax income	100.0	6.6	17.9	17.6	10.0	47.9	27.2	20.7
Share of total spending	100.0	7.9	19.4	18.5	10.1	44.1	25.7	18.4
TRAVEL	100.0	3.3	12.2	14.7	8.5	61.3	33.5	27.8
Airline fares	100.0	3.3	10.3	14.0	6.2	66.2	35.6	30.7
Alcoholic beverages purchased on trips	100.0	2.4	10.1	16.7	7.2	63.5	36.6	26.9
Bus fares, intercity	100.0	10.8	13.8	15.9	7.5	52.0	28.1	23.9
Gasoline and motor oil on trips	100.0	4.9	15.5	19.3	11.4	49.0	29.8	19.2
Groceries on trips	100.0	4.6	13.2	18.7	10.2	53.3	28.9	24.4
Lodging on trips	100.0	2.4	11.8	13.2	9.0	63.7	33.4	30.3
Luggage	100.0	5.3	23.5	15.9	8.7	46.0	30.7	15.3
Parking fees and tolls on trips	100.0	2.9	12.5	13.5	11.6	59.5	33.0	26.5
Recreational expenses on trips	100.0	3.2	12.5	14.4	9.2	60.7	35.5	25.3
Restaurants and carry-outs on trips	100.0	3.0	13.1	14.9	8.9	60.1	33.1	26.9
Ship fares	100.0	5.4	13.3	11.3	10.1	59.8	32.1	27.6
Taxis and local transportation on trips	100.0	3.0	9.5	12.0	6.6	68.9	38.7	30.2
Train fares, intercity	100.0	1.2	9.6	12.5	5.6	71.2	32.3	38.9
Vehicle rental on trips	100.0	1.2	10.8	15.5	7.6	65.0	32.9	32.0

Note: Numbers may not add to total because of rounding.
Source: Calculations by New Strategist based on the Bureau of Labor Statistics' 2012 Consumer Expenditure Survey

Airline Fares

Best customers:
Householders aged 45 to 64
Married couples without children at home
Married couples with school-aged or older children at home
Asians
Households in the West and Northeast
College graduates

Customer trends:
Average household spending on airline fares may continue to grow as boomers retire and devote more money to travel.

The biggest spenders on airline fares are college-educated middle-aged or older adults. Householders ranging in age from 45 to 64 spend 23 to 31 percent more than average on airfares and account for nearly half the market. College graduates spend over twice the average on airfares and account for two-thirds of the market. Married couples without children at home (most of them empty-nesters) spend 53 percent more than average on airfares, while those with school-aged or older children at home spend 52 to 55 percent more than average on this item. Asians spend almost three times the average on airfares. Households in the West and Northeast spend 38 and 27 percent more than average, respectively.

Average household spending on airline fares has been on a rollercoaster ride. Spending on airfares rose 4 percent from 2000 to the overall peak spending year of 2006, fell 10 percent between then and the overall trough spending year of 2010, and increased 3 percent between 2010 and 2012, after adjusting for inflation. Behind the decline was the Great Recession, which reduced spending on travel. Average household spending on airline fares may continue to grow as boomers retire and devote more money to travel.

Table 32. Airline fares

Total household spending	$43,860,372,480.00
Average household spends	352.53

	AVERAGE HOUSEHOLD SPENDING	BEST CUSTOMERS (index)	BIGGEST CUSTOMERS (market share)
AGE OF HOUSEHOLDER			
Average household	**$352.53**	**100**	**100.0%**
Under age 25	157.82	45	2.9
Aged 25 to 34	299.42	85	13.7
Aged 35 to 44	328.25	93	16.2
Aged 45 to 54	433.37	123	24.3
Aged 55 to 64	463.30	131	24.1
Aged 65 to 74	386.59	110	13.2
Aged 75 or older	200.99	57	5.6

	AVERAGE HOUSEHOLD SPENDING	BEST CUSTOMERS (index)	BIGGEST CUSTOMERS (market share)
HOUSEHOLD INCOME			
Average household	**$352.53**	**100**	**100.0%**
Under $20,000	95.67	27	5.7
$20,000 to $39,999	140.67	40	9.0
$40,000 to $49,999	194.06	55	4.9
$50,000 to $69,999	305.61	87	12.5
$70,000 to $79,999	363.05	103	5.7
$80,000 to $99,999	426.10	121	10.7
$100,000 or more	969.51	275	51.5
HOUSEHOLD TYPE			
Average household	**352.53**	**100**	**100.0**
Married couples	510.99	145	70.4
Married couples, no children	540.00	153	31.9
Married couples with children	510.34	145	34.0
Oldest child under age 6	390.95	111	5.1
Oldest child aged 6 to 17	534.99	152	18.0
Oldest child aged 18 or older	546.01	155	10.9
Single parent with child under age 18	132.19	37	2.0
Single person	208.54	59	17.6
RACE AND HISPANIC ORIGIN			
Average household	**352.53**	**100**	**100.0**
Asian	986.90	280	12.1
Black	150.78	43	5.4
Hispanic	217.24	62	7.7
Non-Hispanic white and other	408.38	116	86.9
REGION			
Average household	**352.53**	**100**	**100.0**
Northeast	447.89	127	22.9
Midwest	304.40	86	19.1
South	253.02	72	26.7
West	487.96	138	31.2
EDUCATION			
Average household	**352.53**	**100**	**100.0**
Less than high school graduate	89.61	25	3.3
High school graduate	145.50	41	10.3
Some college	238.86	68	14.0
Associate's degree	221.63	63	6.2
Bachelor's degree or more	740.27	210	66.2
Bachelor's degree	628.98	178	35.6
Master's, professional, doctoral degree	931.39	264	30.7

Note: Market shares may not sum to 100.0 because of rounding and missing categories by household type. "Asian" and "black" include Hispanics and non-Hispanics who identify themselves as being of the respective race alone. "Hispanic" includes people of any race who identify themselves as Hispanic. "Other" includes people who identify themselves as non-Hispanic and as Alaska Native, American Indian, Asian (who are also included in the "Asian" row), or Native Hawaiian or other Pacific Islander, as well as non-Hispanics reporting more than one race.
Source: Calculations by New Strategist based on the Bureau of Labor Statistics' 2012 Consumer Expenditure Survey

Alcoholic Beverages Purchased on Trips

Best customers:	**Householders aged 55 to 64**
	Married couples without children at home
	Non-Hispanic whites
	Households in the West
	College graduates
Customer trends:	**Average household spending on alcoholic beverages purchased on trips should begin to grow again as boomers retire and spend more time and money traveling.**

The biggest spenders on alcoholic beverages purchased on trips can be found in a variety of demographic categories. Householders aged 55 to 64 spend 20 percent more than average on this item. Married couples without children at home (most of them older) spend 77 percent more than average on alcoholic beverages while on trips. These empty-nesters spend more than other household types on alcoholic beverages while traveling because they no longer need to devote their time and money to children's wants and needs. Non-Hispanic whites spend 19 percent more than average on alcoholic beverages while traveling and constitute 90 percent of the market. Households in the West spend 19 percent more than average on alcohol while traveling. College graduates spend twice the average on this item.

Average household spending on alcoholic beverages purchased on trips grew by 8 percent between 2000 and 2006, after adjusting for inflation, then fell 11 percent between 2006 and 2012. Behind the decline was the Great Recession, which reduced spending on travel. In the years ahead, spending on this item should rise again as boomers retire and spend more time and money traveling.

Table 33. Alcoholic beverages purchased on trips

Total household spending	$5,449,420,800.00
Average household spends	43.80

	AVERAGE HOUSEHOLD SPENDING	BEST CUSTOMERS (index)	BIGGEST CUSTOMERS (market share)
AGE OF HOUSEHOLDER			
Average household	**$43.80**	**100**	**100.0%**
Under age 25	22.58	52	3.4
Aged 25 to 34	49.77	114	18.4
Aged 35 to 44	44.83	102	17.8
Aged 45 to 54	48.53	111	21.9
Aged 55 to 64	52.39	120	21.9
Aged 65 to 74	43.50	99	12.0
Aged 75 or older	21.08	48	4.7

	AVERAGE HOUSEHOLD SPENDING	BEST CUSTOMERS (index)	BIGGEST CUSTOMERS (market share)
HOUSEHOLD INCOME			
Average household	**$43.80**	**100**	**100.0%**
Under $20,000	10.62	24	5.1
$20,000 to $39,999	14.22	32	7.3
$40,000 to $49,999	27.11	62	5.5
$50,000 to $69,999	36.90	84	12.2
$70,000 to $79,999	42.62	97	5.4
$80,000 to $99,999	68.80	157	13.9
$100,000 or more	118.51	271	50.7
HOUSEHOLD TYPE			
Average household	**43.80**	**100**	**100.0**
Married couples	59.60	136	66.1
Married couples, no children	77.66	177	37.0
Married couples with children	48.43	111	26.0
Oldest child under age 6	49.77	114	5.2
Oldest child aged 6 to 17	49.47	113	13.4
Oldest child aged 18 or older	45.79	105	7.4
Single parent with child under age 18	14.50	33	1.7
Single person	29.67	68	20.1
RACE AND HISPANIC ORIGIN			
Average household	**43.80**	**100**	**100.0**
Asian	37.59	86	3.7
Black	14.51	33	4.2
Hispanic	21.94	50	6.3
Non-Hispanic white and other	52.29	119	89.6
REGION			
Average household	**43.80**	**100**	**100.0**
Northeast	47.75	109	19.7
Midwest	44.25	101	22.4
South	36.64	84	31.2
West	52.05	119	26.8
EDUCATION			
Average household	**43.80**	**100**	**100.0**
Less than high school graduate	8.20	19	2.4
High school graduate	17.72	40	10.1
Some college	35.62	81	16.7
Associate's degree	32.09	73	7.2
Bachelor's degree or more	88.17	201	63.5
Bachelor's degree	80.37	183	36.6
Master's, professional, doctoral degree	101.58	232	26.9

Note: Market shares may not sum to 100.0 because of rounding and missing categories by household type. "Asian" and "black" include Hispanics and non-Hispanics who identify themselves as being of the respective race alone. "Hispanic" includes people of any race who identify themselves as Hispanic. "Other" includes people who identify themselves as non-Hispanic and as Alaska Native, American Indian, Asian (who are also included in the "Asian" row), or Native Hawaiian or other Pacific Islander, as well as non-Hispanics reporting more than one race.
Source: Calculations by New Strategist based on the Bureau of Labor Statistics' 2012 Consumer Expenditure Survey

Bus Fares, Intercity

Best customers: Householders aged 55 to 74
                             Married couples without children at home
                             Married couples with adult children at home
                             Asians
                             Households in the Northeast and West

Customer trends: Average household spending on intercity bus fares should stabilize as travelers
                             look for less expensive ways to get from point A to point B.

The best customers of intercity bus fares are older householders in the Northeast and West and households with adult children. Householders aged 55 to 74 spend 21 to 45 percent more than average on intercity bus fares. Married couples with adult children at home spend 48 percent more than average on this item, many of them paying for their college-aged children to go to and from school. Married couples without children at home spend 68 percent more than average on bus fares and control 35 percent of the market. Asian households spend twice the average on intercity bus travel. Households in the Northeast spend 17 percent more than average on this item, and households in the West spend 13 percent more.

Average household spending on intercity bus fares fell by a substantial 49 percent between 2000 and 2010, after adjusting for inflation, then rebounded by 10 percent between 2010 and 2012. Behind the decline were the Great Recession and the reduction in travel spending as well as discounters offering lower-cost bus travel along well-traveled routes. Average household spending on intercity bus fares should stabilize as travelers look for less expensive ways to get from point A to point B.

Table 34. Bus fares, intercity

Total household spending	$1,488,015,360.00
Average household spends	11.96

	AVERAGE HOUSEHOLD SPENDING	BEST CUSTOMERS (index)	BIGGEST CUSTOMERS (market share)
AGE OF HOUSEHOLDER			
Average household	**$11.96**	**100**	**100.0%**
Under age 25	5.94	50	3.3
Aged 25 to 34	9.10	76	12.3
Aged 35 to 44	9.97	83	14.5
Aged 45 to 54	13.28	111	22.0
Aged 55 to 64	14.45	121	22.1
Aged 65 to 74	17.31	145	17.4
Aged 75 or older	10.37	87	8.5

	AVERAGE HOUSEHOLD SPENDING	BEST CUSTOMERS (index)	BIGGEST CUSTOMERS (market share)
HOUSEHOLD INCOME			
Average household	**$11.96**	**100**	**100.0%**
Under $20,000	6.29	53	11.1
$20,000 to $39,999	7.03	59	13.2
$40,000 to $49,999	6.91	58	5.1
$50,000 to $69,999	12.90	108	15.6
$70,000 to $79,999	13.80	115	6.4
$80,000 to $99,999	17.17	144	12.7
$100,000 or more	22.95	192	35.9
HOUSEHOLD TYPE			
Average household	**11.96**	**100**	**100.0**
Married couples	16.30	136	66.2
Married couples, no children	20.13	168	35.1
Married couples with children	12.83	107	25.2
Oldest child under age 6	9.04	76	3.4
Oldest child aged 6 to 17	11.38	95	11.3
Oldest child aged 18 or older	17.73	148	10.5
Single parent with child under age 18	4.74	40	2.1
Single person	7.92	66	19.7
RACE AND HISPANIC ORIGIN			
Average household	**11.96**	**100**	**100.0**
Asian	23.87	200	8.7
Black	8.73	73	9.2
Hispanic	11.51	96	12.1
Non-Hispanic white and other	12.60	105	79.1
REGION			
Average household	**11.96**	**100**	**100.0**
Northeast	13.94	117	21.0
Midwest	11.13	93	20.6
South	10.57	88	32.9
West	13.52	113	25.5
EDUCATION			
Average household	**11.96**	**100**	**100.0**
Less than high school graduate	9.90	83	10.8
High school graduate	6.62	55	13.8
Some college	9.25	77	15.9
Associate's degree	9.06	76	7.5
Bachelor's degree or more	19.73	165	52.0
Bachelor's degree	16.89	141	28.1
Master's, professional, doctoral degree	24.61	206	23.9

Note: Market shares may not sum to 100.0 because of rounding and missing categories by household type. "Asian" and "black" include Hispanics and non-Hispanics who identify themselves as being of the respective race alone. "Hispanic" includes people of any race who identify themselves as Hispanic. "Other" includes people who identify themselves as non-Hispanic and as Alaska Native, American Indian, Asian (who are also included in the "Asian" row), or Native Hawaiian or other Pacific Islander, as well as non-Hispanics reporting more than one race.
Source: Calculations by New Strategist based on the Bureau of Labor Statistics' 2012 Consumer Expenditure Survey

Gasoline and Motor Oil on Trips

Best customers: Householders aged 45 to 74
                        Married couples
                        Households in the Midwest and West

Customer trends: Average household spending on gasoline and motor oil on trips should rise
                        in the next few years as more boomers fill the peak traveling lifestage.

Because gasoline (and motor oil) are such commonly purchased items, variations in spending across most demographic categories are relatively small. The biggest spenders on gasoline purchased while traveling are the largest households as well as the most avid travelers— empty-nesters. Householders aged 45 to 74 spend 12 to 19 percent more than average on this item. Married couples without children at home (most of them empty-nesters) spend 67 percent more than average on gasoline and motor oil while traveling and account for over one-third of the market. Couples with children at home spend 37 percent more than average on this item, the figure peaking among those with school-aged children at 47 percent. Households in the Midwest and West outspend the average by 14 to 16 percent.

Average household spending on gasoline and motor oil on trips rose 19 percent between 2000 and the overall peak spending year of 2006, after adjusting for inflation, as gas prices increased. Spending then fell 15 percent between 2006 and 2010 as the Great Recession took hold and gas prices eased slightly, but rebounded strongly with a 19 percent rise between 2010 and 2012. Average household spending on gasoline and motor oil while traveling should rise in the next few years as more boomers fill the peak traveling lifestage.

Table 35. Gasoline and motor oil on trips

Total household spending	$18,534,251,520.00
Average household spends	148.97

	AVERAGE HOUSEHOLD SPENDING	BEST CUSTOMERS (index)	BIGGEST CUSTOMERS (market share)
AGE OF HOUSEHOLDER			
Average household	**$148.97**	**100**	**100.0%**
Under age 25	74.71	50	3.3
Aged 25 to 34	146.97	99	15.9
Aged 35 to 44	155.27	104	18.1
Aged 45 to 54	167.28	112	22.2
Aged 55 to 64	176.77	119	21.7
Aged 65 to 74	170.19	114	13.8
Aged 75 or older	75.58	51	5.0

	AVERAGE HOUSEHOLD SPENDING	BEST CUSTOMERS (index)	BIGGEST CUSTOMERS (market share)
HOUSEHOLD INCOME			
Average household	**$148.97**	**100**	**100.0%**
Under $20,000	49.34	33	7.0
$20,000 to $39,999	93.53	63	14.2
$40,000 to $49,999	119.34	80	7.1
$50,000 to $69,999	152.37	102	14.8
$70,000 to $79,999	211.58	142	7.9
$80,000 to $99,999	243.86	164	14.4
$100,000 or more	275.65	185	34.6
HOUSEHOLD TYPE			
Average household	**148.97**	**100**	**100.0**
Married couples	219.03	147	71.4
Married couples, no children	248.26	167	34.7
Married couples with children	204.32	137	32.2
Oldest child under age 6	191.67	129	5.9
Oldest child aged 6 to 17	218.48	147	17.4
Oldest child aged 18 or older	188.62	127	8.9
Single parent with child under age 18	73.56	49	2.6
Single person	74.07	50	14.8
RACE AND HISPANIC ORIGIN			
Average household	**148.97**	**100**	**100.0**
Asian	111.56	75	3.2
Black	73.29	49	6.2
Hispanic	91.51	61	7.7
Non-Hispanic white and other	171.03	115	86.2
REGION			
Average household	**148.97**	**100**	**100.0**
Northeast	107.03	72	13.0
Midwest	169.99	114	25.3
South	141.98	95	35.5
West	173.43	116	26.2
EDUCATION			
Average household	**148.97**	**100**	**100.0**
Less than high school graduate	56.09	38	4.9
High school graduate	92.48	62	15.5
Some college	139.28	93	19.3
Associate's degree	171.42	115	11.4
Bachelor's degree or more	231.37	155	49.0
Bachelor's degree	222.88	150	29.8
Master's, professional, doctoral degree	245.96	165	19.2

Note: Market shares may not sum to 100.0 because of rounding and missing categories by household type. "Asian" and "black" include Hispanics and non-Hispanics who identify themselves as being of the respective race alone. "Hispanic" includes people of any race who identify themselves as Hispanic. "Other" includes people who identify themselves as non-Hispanic and as Alaska Native, American Indian, Asian (who are also included in the "Asian" row), or Native Hawaiian or other Pacific Islander, as well as non-Hispanics reporting more than one race.
Source: Calculations by New Strategist based on the Bureau of Labor Statistics' 2012 Consumer Expenditure Survey

Groceries on Trips

Best customers: Householders aged 45 to 74
                         Married couples without children at home
                         Married couples with school-aged children
                         Households in the West

Customer trends: Average household spending on groceries while traveling should rise in
                         the next few years as boomers retire.

The biggest spenders on groceries purchased on trips are older married couples, the most avid travelers. These couples are stocking up on food and drink for their hotel rooms or RVs. Householders ranging in age from 45 to 74 spend 28 to 32 percent more than average on this item. Married couples without children at home (most of them empty-nesters) spend 78 percent more than average on groceries while traveling and account for 37 percent of the market. Couples with school-aged children spend 55 percent more. Households in the West spend 31 percent more than average on groceries while traveling.

Average household spending on groceries while traveling grew 10 percent between 2010 and 2012, after adjusting for inflation. It had fallen 14 percent in the 10 years before that time. One factor behind the decline was the reduction in travel spending because of the Great Recession. Average household spending on groceries while traveling should rise in the next few years as boomers retire.

Table 36. Groceries on trips

Total household spending	$6,249,415,680.00
Average household spends	50.23

	AVERAGE HOUSEHOLD SPENDING	BEST CUSTOMERS (index)	BIGGEST CUSTOMERS (market share)
AGE OF HOUSEHOLDER			
Average household	**$50.23**	**100**	**100.0%**
Under age 25	8.36	17	1.1
Aged 25 to 34	39.51	79	12.7
Aged 35 to 44	47.04	94	16.3
Aged 45 to 54	66.42	132	26.2
Aged 55 to 64	64.15	128	23.4
Aged 65 to 74	65.21	130	15.6
Aged 75 or older	24.43	49	4.8

	AVERAGE HOUSEHOLD SPENDING	BEST CUSTOMERS (index)	BIGGEST CUSTOMERS (market share)
HOUSEHOLD INCOME			
Average household	**$50.23**	**100**	**100.0%**
Under $20,000	15.50	31	6.5
$20,000 to $39,999	27.90	56	12.5
$40,000 to $49,999	33.07	66	5.8
$50,000 to $69,999	43.13	86	12.4
$70,000 to $79,999	67.71	135	7.5
$80,000 to $99,999	79.43	158	14.0
$100,000 or more	110.76	221	41.3
HOUSEHOLD TYPE			
Average household	**50.23**	**100**	**100.0**
Married couples	74.10	148	71.7
Married couples, no children	89.21	178	37.0
Married couples with children	66.03	131	30.9
Oldest child under age 6	45.26	90	4.1
Oldest child aged 6 to 17	77.90	155	18.4
Oldest child aged 18 or older	59.45	118	8.4
Single parent with child under age 18	26.05	52	2.7
Single person	23.77	47	14.1
RACE AND HISPANIC ORIGIN			
Average household	**50.23**	**100**	**100.0**
Asian	53.06	106	4.6
Black	18.58	37	4.6
Hispanic	28.60	57	7.1
Non-Hispanic white and other	59.08	118	88.3
REGION			
Average household	**50.23**	**100**	**100.0**
Northeast	50.20	100	18.0
Midwest	44.88	89	19.8
South	44.01	88	32.6
West	65.81	131	29.5
EDUCATION			
Average household	**50.23**	**100**	**100.0**
Less than high school graduate	17.76	35	4.6
High school graduate	26.69	53	13.2
Some college	45.50	91	18.7
Associate's degree	51.76	103	10.2
Bachelor's degree or more	84.90	169	53.3
Bachelor's degree	72.82	145	28.9
Master's, professional, doctoral degree	105.63	210	24.4

Note: Market shares may not sum to 100.0 because of rounding and missing categories by household type. "Asian" and "black" include Hispanics and non-Hispanics who identify themselves as being of the respective race alone. "Hispanic" includes people of any race who identify themselves as Hispanic. "Other" includes people who identify themselves as non-Hispanic and as Alaska Native, American Indian, Asian (who are also included in the "Asian" row), or Native Hawaiian or other Pacific Islander, as well as non-Hispanics reporting more than one race.
Source: Calculations by New Strategist based on the Bureau of Labor Statistics' 2012 Consumer Expenditure Survey

Local Transportation on Trips

Best customers: Householders aged 55 to 74

High-income households

Married couples without children at home

Married couples with adult children at home

Asians and non-Hispanic whites

Households in the Northeast

College graduates

Customer trends: Average household spending on local transportation on trips should rise
as more boomers retire and become avid travelers.

Older married couples and the affluent spend the most on local transportation on trips, a category that includes taxi fares and limousine service. Householders ranging in age from 55 to 74 spend 28 to 39 percent more than average on this item. Married couples without children at home (most of them empty-nesters) spend 73 percent more than average on local transportation on trips, and those with adult children at home spend 64 percent more. High-income households spend more than three times the average on this item, while college graduates and Asians (each an affluent demographic) spend twice the average. Non-Hispanic whites spend 15 percent more on this item. Households in the Northeast spend 46 percent more than average on local transportation on trips.

Average household spending on local transportation on trips rose slowly in the first part of the decade, after adjusting for inflation, then declined 25 percent between 2006 and 2010 and has stagnated since then. Average household spending on local transportation on trips should rise as more boomers retire and become avid travelers.

Table 37. Local transportation on trips

Total household spending $2,215,848,960.00
Average household spends   17.81

	AVERAGE HOUSEHOLD SPENDING	BEST CUSTOMERS (index)	BIGGEST CUSTOMERS (market share)
AGE OF HOUSEHOLDER			
Average household	**$17.81**	**100**	**100.0%**
Under age 25	6.94	39	2.6
Aged 25 to 34	14.84	83	13.5
Aged 35 to 44	15.02	84	14.6
Aged 45 to 54	20.40	115	22.7
Aged 55 to 64	24.81	139	25.5
Aged 65 to 74	22.72	128	15.4
Aged 75 or older	10.57	59	5.8

	AVERAGE HOUSEHOLD SPENDING	BEST CUSTOMERS (index)	BIGGEST CUSTOMERS (market share)
HOUSEHOLD INCOME			
Average household	**$17.81**	**100**	**100.0%**
Under $20,000	3.54	20	4.2
$20,000 to $39,999	5.55	31	7.0
$40,000 to $49,999	6.11	34	3.0
$50,000 to $69,999	16.08	90	13.0
$70,000 to $79,999	15.04	84	4.7
$80,000 to $99,999	18.24	102	9.0
$100,000 or more	56.11	315	59.0
HOUSEHOLD TYPE			
Average household	**17.81**	**100**	**100.0**
Married couples	25.51	143	69.6
Married couples, no children	30.83	173	36.1
Married couples with children	22.71	128	30.0
Oldest child under age 6	21.00	118	5.4
Oldest child aged 6 to 17	19.53	110	13.0
Oldest child aged 18 or older	29.19	164	11.6
Single parent with child under age 18	7.89	44	2.3
Single person	11.52	65	19.2
RACE AND HISPANIC ORIGIN			
Average household	**17.81**	**100**	**100.0**
Asian	36.27	204	8.8
Black	9.38	53	6.6
Hispanic	9.89	56	7.0
Non-Hispanic white and other	20.53	115	86.5
REGION			
Average household	**17.81**	**100**	**100.0**
Northeast	26.01	146	26.4
Midwest	15.03	84	18.7
South	13.54	76	28.3
West	21.03	118	26.6
EDUCATION			
Average household	**17.81**	**100**	**100.0**
Less than high school graduate	4.13	23	3.0
High school graduate	6.78	38	9.5
Some college	10.41	58	12.0
Associate's degree	11.85	67	6.6
Bachelor's degree or more	38.90	218	68.9
Bachelor's degree	34.59	194	38.7
Master's, professional, doctoral degree	46.32	260	30.2

Note: Market shares may not sum to 100.0 because of rounding and missing categories by household type. "Asian" and "black" include Hispanics and non-Hispanics who identify themselves as being of the respective race alone. "Hispanic" includes people of any race who identify themselves as Hispanic. "Other" includes people who identify themselves as non-Hispanic and as Alaska Native, American Indian, Asian (who are also included in the "Asian" row), or Native Hawaiian or other Pacific Islander, as well as non-Hispanics reporting more than one race.
Source: Calculations by New Strategist based on the Bureau of Labor Statistics' 2012 Consumer Expenditure Survey

Lodging on Trips

Best customers: Householders aged 45 to 74
Married couples without children at home
Married couples with school-aged or older children at home
Asians and non-Hispanic whites
College graduates

Customer trends: Average household spending on lodging should grow as boomers retire
and spend more time and money traveling.

Lodging, the second-biggest travel expense after airline fares, accounts for 23 percent of all household travel spending. The biggest spenders on lodging are the most avid travelers—middle-aged and older empty-nesters. Householders ranging in age from 45 to 74 spend 25 to 35 percent more than average on this item and account for 65 percent of the market. Married couples without children at home (most of them empty-nesters) spend 78 percent more than average on lodging. Couples with school-aged or older children at home spend 44 to 56 percent more than the average household on lodging on trips. Non-Hispanic whites spend 21 percent more than average on lodging and Asians spend 16 percent more. College graduates spend twice the average on lodging while traveling.

Average household spending on lodging climbed by 9 percent between 2000 and the overall peak spending year of 2006, after adjusting for inflation. Spending on this item then declined 14 percent between 2006 and 2010 as the Great Recession took hold. Spending on lodging rebounded in the two years following the overall trough spending year of 2010, rising by 8 percent. Average household spending on lodging should grow as boomers retire and spend more time and money traveling.

Table 38. Lodging on trips

Total household spending $42,501,749,760.00
Average household spends 341.61

AGE OF HOUSEHOLDER	AVERAGE HOUSEHOLD SPENDING	BEST CUSTOMERS (index)	BIGGEST CUSTOMERS (market share)
Average household	**$341.61**	**100**	**100.0%**
Under age 25	83.10	24	1.6
Aged 25 to 34	246.44	72	11.7
Aged 35 to 44	317.22	93	16.1
Aged 45 to 54	427.72	125	24.8
Aged 55 to 64	438.71	128	23.5
Aged 65 to 74	460.65	135	16.2
Aged 75 or older	212.82	62	6.1

	AVERAGE HOUSEHOLD SPENDING	BEST CUSTOMERS (index)	BIGGEST CUSTOMERS (market share)
HOUSEHOLD INCOME			
Average household	**$341.61**	**100**	**100.0%**
Under $20,000	81.37	24	5.0
$20,000 to $39,999	126.48	37	8.3
$40,000 to $49,999	189.82	56	4.9
$50,000 to $69,999	243.26	71	10.3
$70,000 to $79,999	424.07	124	6.9
$80,000 to $99,999	450.83	132	11.6
$100,000 or more	964.61	282	52.9
HOUSEHOLD TYPE			
Average household	**341.61**	**100**	**100.0**
Married couples	523.87	153	74.5
Married couples, no children	609.63	178	37.2
Married couples with children	481.03	141	33.1
Oldest child under age 6	327.60	96	4.4
Oldest child aged 6 to 17	534.01	156	18.6
Oldest child aged 18 or older	490.94	144	10.1
Single parent with child under age 18	138.18	40	2.1
Single person	161.26	47	14.0
RACE AND HISPANIC ORIGIN			
Average household	**341.61**	**100**	**100.0**
Asian	397.20	116	5.0
Black	142.16	42	5.2
Hispanic	114.68	34	4.2
Non-Hispanic white and other	412.30	121	90.6
REGION			
Average household	**341.61**	**100**	**100.0**
Northeast	381.23	112	20.1
Midwest	328.23	96	21.3
South	294.30	86	32.1
West	401.22	117	26.5
EDUCATION			
Average household	**341.61**	**100**	**100.0**
Less than high school graduate	61.66	18	2.4
High school graduate	161.62	47	11.8
Some college	218.36	64	13.2
Associate's degree	310.87	91	9.0
Bachelor's degree or more	689.92	202	63.7
Bachelor's degree	572.12	167	33.4
Master's, professional, doctoral degree	892.23	261	30.3

Note: Market shares may not sum to 100.0 because of rounding and missing categories by household type. "Asian" and "black" include Hispanics and non-Hispanics who identify themselves as being of the respective race alone. "Hispanic" includes people of any race who identify themselves as Hispanic. "Other" includes people who identify themselves as non-Hispanic and as Alaska Native, American Indian, Asian (who are also included in the "Asian" row), or Native Hawaiian or other Pacific Islander, as well as non-Hispanics reporting more than one race.
Source: Calculations by New Strategist based on the Bureau of Labor Statistics' 2012 Consumer Expenditure Survey

Luggage

Best customers:	**Householders aged 35 to 44 and 55 to 64**
	Married couples without children at home
	Married couples with children under age 18
	Single parents
Customer trends:	**Average household spending on luggage is likely to stabilize along with college enrollment, although the growing number of boomer travelers may boost it a bit more.**

The biggest spenders on luggage are middle-aged parents (with children going to college) and older householders (the most avid travelers). Householders aged 35 to 44, many with children, spend 48 percent more than average on this item. Married couples with children aged 6 to 17 spend twice the average on luggage. Single parents, whose spending approaches average on only a few items, spend 6 percent more than average on luggage. Householders aged 55 to 64 spend one-third more than average on luggage. Married couples without children at home (most older empty-nesters) outspend the average by 34 percent.

Average household spending on luggage grew 24 percent between 2000 and 2012, after adjusting for inflation, including a 4 percent increase from 2010 to 2012. One factor behind the increase in spending on luggage is the growing share of young adults who are going to college, requiring luggage for their travel to and from school. Average household spending on luggage is likely to stabilize along with college enrollment, although retiring boomers may boost it a bit more.

Table 39. Luggage

Total household spending	**$1,715,696,640.00**
Average household spends	**13.79**

	AVERAGE HOUSEHOLD SPENDING	BEST CUSTOMERS (index)	BIGGEST CUSTOMERS (market share)
AGE OF HOUSEHOLDER			
Average household	**$13.79**	**100**	**100.0%**
Under age 25	6.95	50	3.3
Aged 25 to 34	16.36	119	19.2
Aged 35 to 44	20.35	148	25.6
Aged 45 to 54	14.51	105	20.8
Aged 55 to 64	18.36	133	24.4
Aged 65 to 74	4.02	29	3.5
Aged 75 or older	4.20	30	3.0

	AVERAGE HOUSEHOLD SPENDING	BEST CUSTOMERS (index)	BIGGEST CUSTOMERS (market share)
HOUSEHOLD INCOME			
Average household	**$13.79**	**100**	**100.0%**
Under $20,000	6.15	45	9.4
$20,000 to $39,999	13.67	99	22.3
$40,000 to $49,999	4.66	34	3.0
$50,000 to $69,999	12.42	90	13.0
$70,000 to $79,999	12.15	88	4.9
$80,000 to $99,999	10.35	75	6.6
$100,000 or more	31.67	230	43.0
HOUSEHOLD TYPE			
Average household	**13.79**	**100**	**100.0**
Married couples	18.40	133	64.8
Married couples, no children	18.51	134	28.0
Married couples with children	21.03	153	35.9
Oldest child under age 6	18.46	134	6.1
Oldest child aged 6 to 17	27.54	200	23.8
Oldest child aged 18 or older	11.77	85	6.0
Single parent with child under age 18	14.67	106	5.6
Single person	6.78	49	14.6
RACE AND HISPANIC ORIGIN			
Average household	**13.79**	**100**	**100.0**
Asian	9.90	72	3.1
Black	6.61	48	6.0
Hispanic	4.90	36	4.5
Non-Hispanic white and other	16.45	119	89.5
REGION			
Average household	**13.79**	**100**	**100.0**
Northeast	15.14	110	19.8
Midwest	13.29	96	21.4
South	13.51	98	36.5
West	13.67	99	22.3
EDUCATION			
Average household	**13.79**	**100**	**100.0**
Less than high school graduate	5.58	40	5.3
High school graduate	13.02	94	23.5
Some college	10.64	77	15.9
Associate's degree	12.16	88	8.7
Bachelor's degree or more	20.10	146	46.0
Bachelor's degree	21.26	154	30.7
Master's, professional, doctoral degree	18.15	132	15.3

Note: Market shares may not sum to 100.0 because of rounding and missing categories by household type. "Asian" and "black" include Hispanics and non-Hispanics who identify themselves as being of the respective race alone. "Hispanic" includes people of any race who identify themselves as Hispanic. "Other" includes people who identify themselves as non-Hispanic and as Alaska Native, American Indian, Asian (who are also included in the "Asian" row), or Native Hawaiian or other Pacific Islander, as well as non-Hispanics reporting more than one race.
Source: Calculations by New Strategist based on the Bureau of Labor Statistics' 2012 Consumer Expenditure Survey

Parking Fees and Tolls on Trips

Best customers:	**Householders aged 55 to 64**
	Married couples without children at home
	Married couples with school-aged children
	Asians
	Households in the Northeast
Customer trends:	**Average household spending on parking fees and tolls on trips should rise as more boomers retire and take up traveling.**

The most avid travelers spend the most on parking fees and tolls on trips. Householders aged 55 to 64 spend 43 percent more than average on this item. Married couples without children at home, most of them empty-nesters, spend 57 percent more than average on parking fees and tolls on trips, and couples with school-aged children spend 55 percent more. Asians spend 31 percent more than average on this item. Households in the Northeast spend 56 percent more than average on parking and tolls on trips because of the many toll roads in the region and the relatively high parking fees in congested Northeastern cities.

Parking fees and tolls on trips is one of only three travel categories in which average household spending continued to decline since the overall trough spending year of 2010. (The others are vehicle rentals and alcoholic beverages.) Spending on parking and tolls had risen 17 percent between 2000 and 2010, after adjusting for inflation, but fell 5 percent between 2010 and 2012. Average household spending on parking fees and tolls on trips should rise as more boomers retire and take up traveling.

Table 40. Parking fees and tolls on trips

Total household spending	$1,395,947,520.00
Average household spends	11.22

	AVERAGE HOUSEHOLD SPENDING	BEST CUSTOMERS (index)	BIGGEST CUSTOMERS (market share)
AGE OF HOUSEHOLDER			
Average household	**$11.22**	**100**	**100.0%**
Under age 25	4.44	40	2.6
Aged 25 to 34	9.97	89	14.4
Aged 35 to 44	11.22	100	17.4
Aged 45 to 54	12.73	113	22.5
Aged 55 to 64	16.00	143	26.1
Aged 65 to 74	12.41	111	13.3
Aged 75 or older	4.30	38	3.7

	AVERAGE HOUSEHOLD SPENDING	BEST CUSTOMERS (index)	BIGGEST CUSTOMERS (market share)
HOUSEHOLD INCOME			
Average household	**$11.22**	**100**	**100.0%**
Under $20,000	2.59	23	4.9
$20,000 to $39,999	4.60	41	9.2
$40,000 to $49,999	6.08	54	4.8
$50,000 to $69,999	11.63	104	15.0
$70,000 to $79,999	14.45	129	7.2
$80,000 to $99,999	17.00	152	13.4
$100,000 or more	27.27	243	45.5
HOUSEHOLD TYPE			
Average household	**11.22**	**100**	**100.0**
Married couples	16.13	144	69.8
Married couples, no children	17.59	157	32.7
Married couples with children	15.16	135	31.8
Oldest child under age 6	14.08	125	5.7
Oldest child aged 6 to 17	17.38	155	18.4
Oldest child aged 18 or older	12.12	108	7.6
Single parent with child under age 18	5.79	52	2.7
Single person	5.81	52	15.4
RACE AND HISPANIC ORIGIN			
Average household	**11.22**	**100**	**100.0**
Asian	14.68	131	5.7
Black	5.06	45	5.7
Hispanic	8.05	72	9.0
Non-Hispanic white and other	12.78	114	85.5
REGION			
Average household	**11.22**	**100**	**100.0**
Northeast	17.48	156	28.1
Midwest	10.48	93	20.7
South	8.85	79	29.4
West	10.84	97	21.8
EDUCATION			
Average household	**11.22**	**100**	**100.0**
Less than high school graduate	2.51	22	2.9
High school graduate	5.62	50	12.5
Some college	7.33	65	13.5
Associate's degree	13.17	117	11.6
Bachelor's degree or more	21.17	189	59.5
Bachelor's degree	18.56	165	33.0
Master's, professional, doctoral degree	25.64	229	26.5

Note: Market shares may not sum to 100.0 because of rounding and missing categories by household type. "Asian" and "black" include Hispanics and non-Hispanics who identify themselves as being of the respective race alone. "Hispanic" includes people of any race who identify themselves as Hispanic. "Other" includes people who identify themselves as non-Hispanic and as Alaska Native, American Indian, Asian (who are also included in the "Asian" row), or Native Hawaiian or other Pacific Islander, as well as non-Hispanics reporting more than one race.
Source: Calculations by New Strategist based on the Bureau of Labor Statistics' 2012 Consumer Expenditure Survey

Recreational Expenses on Trips

Best customers: Householders aged 45 to 64
   Married couples without children at home
   Married couples with school-aged or older children at home
   Asians and non-Hispanic whites
   Households in the West

Customer trends: Average household spending on recreational expenses on trips should grow
   as boomers retire and spend more time and money on travel.

Recreational expenses on trips, the fifth-largest travel category, account for 9 percent of the average household's travel budget. The biggest spenders on recreational expenses on trips are older married couples. Householders ranging in age from 45 to 64 spend 29 to 33 percent more than average on this item. Married couples without children at home (most of them empty-nesters) spend 56 percent more than average on recreational expenses on trips, while those with school-aged children spend more than twice the average. Asians, who have the highest incomes among racial and ethnic groups, spend 42 percent more than average on recreational expenses on trips. Non-Hispanic whites spend 21 percent more. Households in the West outspend the average on this item by 32 percent.

Average household spending on recreational expenses on trips fell by a steep 34 percent between 2000 and the overall trough spending year of 2010, after adjusting for inflation. Behind the decline was the economic downturn, which reduced spending on travel. In contrast to many other travel categories, however, spending on this item so far has failed to recover. Average household spending on recreational expenses while traveling should grow as boomers retire and spend more time and money on travel.

Table 41. Recreational expenses on trips

Total household spending	$15,986,211,840.00
Average household spends	128.49

	AVERAGE HOUSEHOLD SPENDING	BEST CUSTOMERS (index)	BIGGEST CUSTOMERS (market share)
AGE OF HOUSEHOLDER			
Average household	**$128.49**	**100**	**100.0%**
Under age 25	42.60	33	2.2
Aged 25 to 34	108.94	85	13.7
Aged 35 to 44	136.18	106	18.4
Aged 45 to 54	170.70	133	26.3
Aged 55 to 64	165.60	129	23.6
Aged 65 to 74	128.87	100	12.1
Aged 75 or older	49.31	38	3.8

	AVERAGE HOUSEHOLD SPENDING	BEST CUSTOMERS (index)	BIGGEST CUSTOMERS (market share)
HOUSEHOLD INCOME			
Average household	**$128.49**	**100**	**100.0%**
Under $20,000	31.45	24	5.1
$20,000 to $39,999	47.18	37	8.3
$40,000 to $49,999	64.96	51	4.5
$50,000 to $69,999	111.35	87	12.5
$70,000 to $79,999	130.54	102	5.7
$80,000 to $99,999	181.94	142	12.5
$100,000 or more	352.89	275	51.4
HOUSEHOLD TYPE			
Average household	**128.49**	**100**	**100.0**
Married couples	195.23	152	73.8
Married couples, no children	200.57	156	32.5
Married couples with children	209.27	163	38.3
Oldest child under age 6	116.10	90	4.1
Oldest child aged 6 to 17	266.00	207	24.6
Oldest child aged 18 or older	173.90	135	9.5
Single parent with child under age 18	57.12	44	2.3
Single person	66.59	52	15.4
RACE AND HISPANIC ORIGIN			
Average household	**128.49**	**100**	**100.0**
Asian	182.80	142	6.2
Black	43.78	34	4.3
Hispanic	52.79	41	5.2
Non-Hispanic white and other	155.17	121	90.6
REGION			
Average household	**128.49**	**100**	**100.0**
Northeast	139.47	109	19.6
Midwest	115.25	90	19.9
South	106.51	83	30.9
West	169.06	132	29.6
EDUCATION			
Average household	**128.49**	**100**	**100.0**
Less than high school graduate	31.80	25	3.2
High school graduate	64.22	50	12.5
Some college	89.74	70	14.4
Associate's degree	119.43	93	9.2
Bachelor's degree or more	247.48	193	60.7
Bachelor's degree	228.64	178	35.5
Master's, professional, doctoral degree	279.85	218	25.3

Note: Market shares may not sum to 100.0 because of rounding and missing categories by household type. "Asian" and "black" include Hispanics and non-Hispanics who identify themselves as being of the respective race alone. "Hispanic" includes people of any race who identify themselves as Hispanic. "Other" includes people who identify themselves as non-Hispanic and as Alaska Native, American Indian, Asian (who are also included in the "Asian" row), or Native Hawaiian or other Pacific Islander, as well as non-Hispanics reporting more than one race.
Source: Calculations by New Strategist based on the Bureau of Labor Statistics' 2012 Consumer Expenditure Survey

Restaurant and Carry-Out Food on Trips

Best customers: Householders aged 45 to 74
                             Married couples without children at home
                             Married couples with school-aged or older children at home
                             Asians and non-Hispanic whites
                             Households in the West

Customer trends: Average household spending on restaurant and carry-out food on trips should
                             grow as boomers retire and devote more time and money to travel.

The biggest spenders on restaurant and carry-out meals on trips are the most avid travelers—older married couples. Householders ranging in age from 45 to 74 spend 18 to 30 percent more than average on this item. Married couples without children at home (most of them empty-nesters) spend 71 percent more than average on restaurant and carry-out meals on trips and control 36 percent of the market. Those with school-aged or older children at home spend 42 to 52 percent more. Asians, the most affluent racial and ethnic group, spend 49 percent more than average on eating out while traveling. Non-Hispanic whites spend 18 percent more. Households in the West outspend the average by 20 percent.

Average household spending on restaurant and carry-out food on trips, the third-largest travel spending category, fell 15 percent between 2006 and the overall trough spending year of 2010, after adjusting for inflation. Behind the decline was household budget cutting in the midst of the Great Recession. Spending on restaurant meals rebounded with a 9 increase between 2010 and 2012. Spending on this item should grow in the years ahead as boomers retire and devote more time and money to travel.

Table 42. Restaurant and carry-out food on trips

Total household spending $31,993,574,400.00
Average household spends   257.15

AGE OF HOUSEHOLDER	AVERAGE HOUSEHOLD SPENDING	BEST CUSTOMERS (index)	BIGGEST CUSTOMERS (market share)
Average household	**$257.15**	**100**	**100.0%**
Under age 25	83.51	32	2.1
Aged 25 to 34	220.41	86	13.9
Aged 35 to 44	243.65	95	16.4
Aged 45 to 54	316.16	123	24.3
Aged 55 to 64	334.87	130	23.8
Aged 65 to 74	302.48	118	14.2
Aged 75 or older	137.46	53	5.2

	AVERAGE HOUSEHOLD SPENDING	BEST CUSTOMERS (index)	BIGGEST CUSTOMERS (market share)
HOUSEHOLD INCOME			
Average household	**$257.15**	**100**	**100.0%**
Under $20,000	64.47	25	5.3
$20,000 to $39,999	103.30	40	9.1
$40,000 to $49,999	157.93	61	5.4
$50,000 to $69,999	206.50	80	11.6
$70,000 to $79,999	312.12	121	6.8
$80,000 to $99,999	382.96	149	13.1
$100,000 or more	669.19	260	48.7
HOUSEHOLD TYPE			
Average household	**257.15**	**100**	**100.0**
Married couples	381.63	148	72.1
Married couples, no children	439.38	171	35.6
Married couples with children	358.93	140	32.8
Oldest child under age 6	267.92	104	4.8
Oldest child aged 6 to 17	390.44	152	18.1
Oldest child aged 18 or older	364.67	142	10.0
Single parent with child under age 18	114.33	44	2.3
Single person	135.77	53	15.7
RACE AND HISPANIC ORIGIN			
Average household	**257.15**	**100**	**100.0**
Asian	384.23	149	6.5
Black	106.44	41	5.2
Hispanic	132.11	51	6.4
Non-Hispanic white and other	302.84	118	88.4
REGION			
Average household	**257.15**	**100**	**100.0**
Northeast	273.45	106	19.2
Midwest	240.97	94	20.8
South	227.86	89	33.0
West	308.42	120	27.0
EDUCATION			
Average household	**257.15**	**100**	**100.0**
Less than high school graduate	58.94	23	3.0
High school graduate	135.57	53	13.1
Some college	186.36	72	14.9
Associate's degree	230.79	90	8.9
Bachelor's degree or more	489.81	190	60.1
Bachelor's degree	427.45	166	33.1
Master's, professional, doctoral degree	596.90	232	26.9

Note: Market shares may not sum to 100.0 because of rounding and missing categories by household type. "Asian" and "black" include Hispanics and non-Hispanics who identify themselves as being of the respective race alone. "Hispanic" includes people of any race who identify themselves as Hispanic. "Other" includes people who identify themselves as non-Hispanic and as Alaska Native, American Indian, Asian (who are also included in the "Asian" row), or Native Hawaiian or other Pacific Islander, as well as non-Hispanics reporting more than one race.
Source: Calculations by New Strategist based on the Bureau of Labor Statistics' 2012 Consumer Expenditure Survey

Ship Fares

Best customers:

Householders aged 55 or older

High-income households

Married couples without children at home

Asians and non-Hispanic whites

Households in the Northeast and West

Customer trends:

Average household spending on ship fares should increase in the years ahead as boomers fill the older age groups.

The biggest spenders on ship fares are well-to-do older Americans. Householders aged 55 to 64 spend 73 percent more than average on this item, and those aged 65 to 74 spend 37 percent more. Even householders aged 75 or older are above-average spenders on ship fares. Together these three age groups account for more than half the market. Households with incomes of $100,000 or more spend almost three-and-one-half times the average on ship fares and control 64 percent of household spending on this item. Married couples without children at home (most of them empty-nesters) spend well more than twice the average on cruises. Non-Hispanic whites spend 20 percent more than average on ship fares, and Asians spend more than twice the average. Households in the Northeast outspend the average by 54 percent, and those in the West spend 24 percent more.

Average household spending on ship fares, which had grown by 28 percent from 2000 to 2006, declined 34 percent between 2006 and the overall trough spending year of 2010, after adjusting for inflation. Behind the decline was the economic downturn, which reduced spending on travel. Spending on this item strongly rebounded between 2010 and 2012, rising 36 percent. Average household spending on ship fares should increase in the years ahead as boomers fill the older age groups.

Table 43. Ship fares

Total household spending $7,033,236,480.00
Average household spends   56.53

	AVERAGE HOUSEHOLD SPENDING	BEST CUSTOMERS (index)	BIGGEST CUSTOMERS (market share)
AGE OF HOUSEHOLDER			
Average household	**$56.53**	**100**	**100.0%**
Under age 25	13.45	24	1.6
Aged 25 to 34	29.30	52	8.4
Aged 35 to 44	44.98	80	13.8
Aged 45 to 54	49.37	87	17.3
Aged 55 to 64	97.58	173	31.6
Aged 65 to 74	77.27	137	16.5
Aged 75 or older	63.03	111	10.9

	AVERAGE HOUSEHOLD SPENDING	BEST CUSTOMERS (index)	BIGGEST CUSTOMERS (market share)
HOUSEHOLD INCOME			
Average household	**$56.53**	**100**	**100.0%**
Under $20,000	4.90	9	1.8
$20,000 to $39,999	21.78	39	8.7
$40,000 to $49,999	33.72	60	5.3
$50,000 to $69,999	28.15	50	7.2
$70,000 to $79,999	20.43	36	2.0
$80,000 to $99,999	69.73	123	10.9
$100,000 or more	193.60	342	64.1
HOUSEHOLD TYPE			
Average household	**56.53**	**100**	**100.0**
Married couples	92.07	163	79.1
Married couples, no children	127.16	225	46.9
Married couples with children	68.10	120	28.3
Oldest child under age 6	46.73	83	3.8
Oldest child aged 6 to 17	70.64	125	14.9
Oldest child aged 18 or older	77.64	137	9.7
Single parent with child under age 18	16.40	29	1.5
Single person	21.64	38	11.4
RACE AND HISPANIC ORIGIN			
Average household	**56.53**	**100**	**100.0**
Asian	119.70	212	9.2
Black	22.08	39	4.9
Hispanic	23.53	42	5.2
Non-Hispanic white and other	67.81	120	90.0
REGION			
Average household	**56.53**	**100**	**100.0**
Northeast	87.16	154	27.8
Midwest	37.10	66	14.6
South	45.02	80	29.7
West	70.14	124	28.0
EDUCATION			
Average household	**56.53**	**100**	**100.0**
Less than high school graduate	23.46	42	5.4
High school graduate	30.25	54	13.3
Some college	31.04	55	11.3
Associate's degree	58.06	103	10.1
Bachelor's degree or more	107.16	190	59.8
Bachelor's degree	91.14	161	32.1
Master's, professional, doctoral degree	134.67	238	27.6

Note: Market shares may not sum to 100.0 because of rounding and missing categories by household type. "Asian" and "black" include Hispanics and non-Hispanics who identify themselves as being of the respective race alone. "Hispanic" includes people of any race who identify themselves as Hispanic. "Other" includes people who identify themselves as non-Hispanic and as Alaska Native, American Indian, Asian (who are also included in the "Asian" row), or Native Hawaiian or other Pacific Islander, as well as non-Hispanics reporting more than one race.
Source: Calculations by New Strategist based on the Bureau of Labor Statistics' 2012 Consumer Expenditure Survey

Train Fares, Intercity

Best customers:
Householders aged 55 to 74
Married couples without children at home
Asians and non-Hispanic whites
Households in the West and Northeast
College graduates

Customer trends:
Average household spending on train fares will resume its decline
unless train service improves.

Older Americans are the best customers of intercity train fares. Householders aged 55 to 64 spend 33 percent more than average on intercity train tickets, and those aged 65 to 74 spend 66 percent more. Married couples without children at home (most of them empty-nesters) spend nearly twice the average on intercity train fares. Asians outspend the average by 76 percent, and non-Hispanic whites spend 19 percent more. Households in the West and Northeast spend, respectively, 28 and 16 percent more than average on train fares. Households headed by people with a bachelor's degree spend more than twice the average on intercity train fares.

Average household spending on intercity train fares had been in a decade-long decline, but it recovered nicely in the last two years. Spending on train fares fell 34 percent between 2000 and 2006, after adjusting for inflation, and by another 11 percent between 2006 and 2010. Then came a big upswing, and average household spending on train fares climbed by a solid 14 percent between 2010 and 2012. Behind the earlier decline is increasingly limited train service in the United States and belt tightening because of the Great Recession. Unless train service improves, the recent upswing in average household spending on train fares will be short-lived.

Table 44. Train fares, intercity

Total household spending $2,348,974,080.00
Average household spends   18.88

	AVERAGE HOUSEHOLD SPENDING	BEST CUSTOMERS (index)	BIGGEST CUSTOMERS (market share)
AGE OF HOUSEHOLDER			
Average household	**$18.88**	**100**	**100.0%**
Under age 25	6.32	33	2.2
Aged 25 to 34	13.05	69	11.2
Aged 35 to 44	15.08	80	13.9
Aged 45 to 54	18.04	96	18.9
Aged 55 to 64	25.04	133	24.3
Aged 65 to 74	31.29	166	20.0
Aged 75 or older	18.55	98	9.6

	AVERAGE HOUSEHOLD SPENDING	BEST CUSTOMERS (index)	BIGGEST CUSTOMERS (market share)
HOUSEHOLD INCOME			
Average household	**$18.88**	**100**	**100.0%**
Under $20,000	10.32	55	11.5
$20,000 to $39,999	7.41	39	8.8
$40,000 to $49,999	14.44	76	6.8
$50,000 to $69,999	13.89	74	10.6
$70,000 to $79,999	15.72	83	4.6
$80,000 to $99,999	13.81	73	6.5
$100,000 or more	51.59	273	51.2
HOUSEHOLD TYPE			
Average household	**18.88**	**100**	**100.0**
Married couples	26.19	139	67.4
Married couples, no children	36.99	196	40.8
Married couples with children	18.20	96	22.7
Oldest child under age 6	15.11	80	3.7
Oldest child aged 6 to 17	18.59	98	11.7
Oldest child aged 18 or older	19.55	104	7.3
Single parent with child under age 18	7.97	42	2.2
Single person	15.54	82	24.4
RACE AND HISPANIC ORIGIN			
Average household	**18.88**	**100**	**100.0**
Asian	33.30	176	7.6
Black	8.31	44	5.5
Hispanic	7.40	39	4.9
Non-Hispanic white and other	22.54	119	89.6
REGION			
Average household	**18.88**	**100**	**100.0**
Northeast	21.95	116	21.0
Midwest	19.01	101	22.3
South	14.10	75	27.8
West	24.19	128	28.9
EDUCATION			
Average household	**18.88**	**100**	**100.0**
Less than high school graduate	1.72	9	1.2
High school graduate	7.24	38	9.6
Some college	11.42	60	12.5
Associate's degree	10.71	57	5.6
Bachelor's degree or more	42.62	226	71.2
Bachelor's degree	30.59	162	32.3
Master's, professional, doctoral degree	63.27	335	38.9

Note: Market shares may not sum to 100.0 because of rounding and missing categories by household type. "Asian" and "black" include Hispanics and non-Hispanics who identify themselves as being of the respective race alone. "Hispanic" includes people of any race who identify themselves as Hispanic. "Other" includes people who identify themselves as non-Hispanic and as Alaska Native, American Indian, Asian (who are also included in the "Asian" row), or Native Hawaiian or other Pacific Islander, as well as non-Hispanics reporting more than one race.
Source: Calculations by New Strategist based on the Bureau of Labor Statistics' 2012 Consumer Expenditure Survey

Vehicle Rentals on Trips

Best customers: Householders aged 45 to 64
High-income households
Married couples without children at home
Married couples with school-aged or older children at home
Asians and non-Hispanic whites
Households in the West
College graduates

Customer trends: Average household spending on vehicle rentals on trips should grow in the years ahead as more boomers retire and become avid travelers.

The biggest spenders on rented vehicles while traveling are middle-aged and older married couples. Householders ranging in age from 45 to 64 spend 24 to 57 percent more than average on this item. Married couples without children at home (most of them empty-nesters) spend 75 percent more than average on vehicle rentals while traveling. Couples with school-aged children spend 45 percent more than average on this item, and those with adult children at home spend 34 percent more. High-income households spend three times the average on vehicle rentals on trips, and college graduates spend two times the average. Asians spend 41 percent more than average and non-Hispanic whites spend 16 percent more. Households in the West spend 27 percent more than average on vehicle rentals while traveling.

Average household spending on vehicle rentals while traveling declined by a steep 41 percent between 2000 and 2010, after adjusting for inflation, and fell by another 6 percent in the two years since then. Price discounting was one factor behind the decline, as was the economic downturn. Average household spending on vehicle rentals while traveling should grow in the years ahead as more boomers retire and become avid travelers.

Table 45. Vehicle rentals on trips

Total household spending	$3,157,678,080.00
Average household spends	25.38

	AVERAGE HOUSEHOLD SPENDING	BEST CUSTOMERS (index)	BIGGEST CUSTOMERS (market share)
AGE OF HOUSEHOLDER			
Average household	**$25.38**	**100**	**100.0%**
Under age 25	6.21	24	1.6
Aged 25 to 34	17.87	70	11.4
Aged 35 to 44	25.80	102	17.6
Aged 45 to 54	31.46	124	24.5
Aged 55 to 64	39.83	157	28.7
Aged 65 to 74	23.98	94	11.4
Aged 75 or older	12.24	48	4.7

	AVERAGE HOUSEHOLD SPENDING	BEST CUSTOMERS (index)	BIGGEST CUSTOMERS (market share)
HOUSEHOLD INCOME			
Average household	**$25.38**	**100**	**100.0%**
Under $20,000	3.68	15	3.1
$20,000 to $39,999	9.76	38	8.7
$40,000 to $49,999	11.56	46	4.0
$50,000 to $69,999	19.21	76	10.9
$70,000 to $79,999	18.53	73	4.1
$80,000 to $99,999	32.73	129	11.4
$100,000 or more	78.60	310	58.0
HOUSEHOLD TYPE			
Average household	**25.38**	**100**	**100.0**
Married couples	37.44	148	71.6
Married couples, no children	44.32	175	36.4
Married couples with children	33.67	133	31.2
Oldest child under age 6	25.16	99	4.5
Oldest child aged 6 to 17	36.81	145	17.2
Oldest child aged 18 or older	33.91	134	9.4
Single parent with child under age 18	10.62	42	2.2
Single person	12.84	51	15.0
RACE AND HISPANIC ORIGIN			
Average household	**25.38**	**100**	**100.0**
Asian	35.77	141	6.1
Black	17.94	71	8.9
Hispanic	7.62	30	3.8
Non-Hispanic white and other	29.53	116	87.3
REGION			
Average household	**25.38**	**100**	**100.0**
Northeast	23.04	91	16.4
Midwest	23.03	91	20.1
South	23.76	94	34.9
West	32.24	127	28.6
EDUCATION			
Average household	**25.38**	**100**	**100.0**
Less than high school graduate	2.36	9	1.2
High school graduate	10.95	43	10.8
Some college	19.09	75	15.5
Associate's degree	19.47	77	7.6
Bachelor's degree or more	52.27	206	65.0
Bachelor's degree	41.93	165	32.9
Master's, professional, doctoral degree	70.02	276	32.0

Note: Market shares may not sum to 100.0 because of rounding and missing categories by household type. "Asian" and "black" include Hispanics and non-Hispanics who identify themselves as being of the respective race alone. "Hispanic" includes people of any race who identify themselves as Hispanic. "Other" includes people who identify themselves as non-Hispanic and as Alaska Native, American Indian, Asian (who are also included in the "Asian" row), or Native Hawaiian or other Pacific Islander, as well as non-Hispanics reporting more than one race.
Source: Calculations by New Strategist based on the Bureau of Labor Statistics' 2012 Consumer Expenditure Survey

Appendix

Spending by Product and Service Ranked by Amount Spent, 2012

(average annual spending of consumer units on products and services, ranked by amount spent, 2012)

1.	Deductions for Social Security	$4,040.62
2.	Groceries (also shown by individual category)	3,920.65
3.	Vehicle purchases (net outlay)	3,210.49
4.	Mortgage interest (or rent, $3,064.09)	2,926.47
5.	Gasoline and motor oil	2,755.78
6.	Restaurants (also shown by meal category)	2,225.50
7.	Health insurance	2,060.78
8.	Property taxes	1,835.60
9.	Federal income taxes	1,568.33
10.	Electricity	1,387.83
11.	Dinner at restaurants	1,082.12
12.	Vehicle insurance	1,017.94
13.	Cellular phone service	861.97
14.	College tuition	824.99
15.	Vehicle maintenance and repairs	814.27
16.	Lunch at restaurants	746.81
17.	Cash contributions to church, religious organizations	734.30
18.	Cable and satellite television services	661.76
19.	Nonpayroll deposit to retirement plans	582.46
20.	Maintenance and repair services, owner	578.78
21.	Women's apparel	572.53
22.	State and local income taxes	526.08
23.	Deductions for private pensions	511.80
24.	Cash gifts to members of other households	464.50
25.	Alcoholic beverages	451.16
26.	Water and sewerage maintenance	398.56
27.	Prescription drugs	366.40
28.	Natural gas	359.35
29.	Residential telephone service and pay phones	358.54
30.	Homeowner's insurance	353.80
31.	Life and other personal insurance	352.61
32.	Airline fares	352.53
33.	Lodging on trips	341.61
34.	Computer information services	336.30
35.	Men's apparel	319.73
36.	Cigarettes	298.75
37.	Personal care services	292.83
38.	Dental services	268.32
39.	Fresh fruits	261.29
40.	Restaurant meals on trips	257.15
41.	Day care centers, nurseries, and preschools	236.56
42.	Cash contributions to charities	233.63
43.	Owned vacation homes	230.28
44.	Breakfast at restaurants	227.60
45.	Beef	226.32
46.	Fresh vegetables	226.14
47.	Vehicle finance charges	223.36
48.	Child support expenditures	208.46
49.	Physician's services	204.16
50.	Pet food	194.70

51.	Finance charges, except mortgage and vehicles	$181.53
52.	Elementary and high school tuition	169.04
53.	Snacks at restaurants	168.97
54.	Movie, theater, amusement park, and other admissions	168.75
55.	Pork	165.77
56.	Computers and computer hardware for nonbusiness use	162.71
57.	Hospital room and services	161.48
58.	Poultry	159.36
59.	Women's footwear	158.87
60.	Leased vehicles	158.68
61.	Cosmetics, perfume, and bath products	157.04
62.	Laundry and cleaning supplies	155.39
63.	Veterinarian services	149.95
64.	Expenses for other properties	149.93
65.	Prepared foods except frozen, salads, and desserts	147.81
66.	Interest paid, home equity loan/line of credit	140.37
67.	Carbonated drinks	139.74
68.	Legal fees	138.71
69.	Pet purchase, supplies, and medicines	135.69
70.	Other taxes	131.96
71.	Housekeeping services	131.93
72.	Cheese	131.47
73.	Fresh milk, all types	128.28
74.	Social, recreation, health club membership	127.44
75.	Household decorative items	126.84
76.	Fish and seafood	125.74
77.	Gardening, lawn care service	125.40
78.	Miscellaneous household products	125.00
79.	Trash and garbage collection	123.44
80.	Fees for participant sports	118.19
81.	Cleansing and toilet tissue, paper towels, and napkins	117.50
82.	Girls' (aged 2 to 15) apparel	115.92
83.	Toys, games, hobbies, and tricycles	114.59
84.	Beer and ale at home	112.49
85.	Men's footwear	111.75
86.	Potato chips and other snacks	111.59
87.	Vehicle registration	111.25
88.	Support for college students	104.82
89.	Wine at home	102.62
90.	Television sets	102.24
91.	Sofas	101.36
92.	Deductions for government retirement	100.54
93.	Nonprescription drugs	97.49
94.	Ready-to-eat and cooked cereals	94.82
95.	Jewelry	94.38
96.	Fees for recreational lessons	92.55
97.	Boys' (aged 2 to 15) apparel	87.96
98.	Candy and chewing gum	87.86
99.	Lunch meats (cold cuts)	87.23
100.	Coffee	86.50
101.	Maintenance and repair materials, owner	86.31
102.	Alimony expenditures	86.01
103.	Babysitting and child care	84.86
104.	Rent as pay	84.60
105.	Fuel oil	80.77
106.	Housing while attending school	76.65
107.	Mattresses and springs	76.43
108.	Lawn and garden supplies	76.04
109.	Beer and ale at bars, restaurants	75.94
110.	Stationery, stationery supplies, giftwrap	75.07

111.	Accounting fees	$75.03
112.	Funeral expenses	72.17
113.	Intracity mass transit fares	71.99
114.	Lawn and garden equipment	71.11
115.	Frozen prepared foods, except meals	70.22
116.	Bedroom linens	67.43
117.	Eyeglasses and contact lenses	66.52
118.	Motorized recreational vehicles	65.66
119.	Admission to sports events	65.45
120.	Books and supplies for college	65.30
121.	Children's (under age 2) apparel	63.31
122.	Bedroom furniture except mattresses and springs	63.24
123.	Service by professionals other than physician	62.38
124.	Hair care products	61.69
125.	Bread, other than white	61.60
126.	Athletic gear, game tables, exercise equipment	60.99
127.	Frozen meals	60.61
128.	Sauces and gravies	60.27
129.	Catered affairs	60.19
130.	Refrigerators and freezers	59.80
131.	School lunches	59.56
132.	Ground rent	58.68
133.	Lottery and gambling losses	57.93
134.	Postage	57.44
135.	Ice cream and related products	57.37
136.	Moving, storage, and freight express	56.88
137.	Bottled water	56.80
138.	Ship fares	56.53
139.	School tuition, books, and supplies other than college, vocational/technical, elementary, high school	55.30
140.	Canned and bottled fruit juice	54.92
141.	Canned vegetables	54.59
142.	Indoor plants and fresh flowers	53.57
143.	Property management, owner	53.28
144.	Eggs	53.08
145.	Other dairy (yogurt, etc.)	52.67
146.	Professional laundry, dry cleaning	52.24
147.	Biscuits and rolls	51.85
148.	Nonprescription vitamins	50.76
149.	Cookies	50.56
150.	Food prepared by consumer unit on trips	50.23
151.	Occupational expenses	48.41
152.	Bottled gas	47.44
153.	Other alcoholic beverages at bars, restaurants	47.43
154.	Lab tests, X-rays	46.91
155.	Canned and packaged soups	46.30
156.	Books	45.30
157.	Board (including at school)	44.93
158.	Alcoholic beverages purchased on trips	43.80
159.	White bread	43.52
160.	Care for elderly, invalids, handicapped, etc.	43.36
161.	Wall units, cabinets, and other furniture	42.39
162.	Nuts	42.35
163.	Parking fees	42.29
164.	Unmotored recreational vehicles	42.12
165.	Eye care services	41.86
166.	Pet services	41.70
167.	Topicals and dressings	40.99
168.	Oral hygiene products	40.82
169.	Coin-operated apparel laundry and dry cleaning	40.21

170.	Newspaper and magazine subscriptions	$39.58
171.	Power tools	39.34
172.	Boys' footwear	39.09
173.	Miscellaneous personal services	38.97
174.	Cash contributions to educational institutions	38.77
175.	Salt, spices, and other seasonings	38.72
176.	Cakes and cupcakes	37.94
177.	Frozen vegetables	37.50
178.	Crackers	37.17
179.	Girls' footwear	37.12
180.	Video game hardware and accessories	37.03
181.	Pasta, cornmeal, and other cereal products	36.98
182.	Fats and oils	36.79
183.	Rented vehicles	36.23
184.	Tolls	35.63
185.	Prepared salads	35.09
186.	Living room chairs	34.57
187.	Care in convalescent or nursing home	34.56
188.	Wine at bars, restaurants	34.54
189.	Deodorants, feminine hygiene, miscellaneous products	34.51
190.	Washing machines	34.12
191.	Sound components, equipment, and accessories	32.07
192.	Kitchen and dining room furniture	31.62
193.	Salad dressings	31.29
194.	Photographic equipment	31.17
195.	Meals as pay	30.79
196.	Tea	30.36
197.	Tobacco products other than cigarettes	30.30
198.	Video cassettes, tapes, and discs	29.70
199.	Jams, preserves, other sweets	29.61
200.	Hunting and fishing equipment	29.06
201.	Frozen and refrigerated bakery products	28.77
202.	Telephones and accessories	27.33
203.	Home security system service fee	27.23
204.	Lamps and lighting fixtures	26.83
205.	Small electric kitchen appliances	25.90
206.	Noncarbonated fruit-flavored drinks	25.83
207.	Butter	25.56
208.	Baby food	25.05
209.	Baking needs	24.95
210.	Cash contributions to political organizations	24.90
211.	Frankfurters	24.71
212.	Rice	24.65
213.	Termite and pest control products and services	24.58
214.	Outdoor equipment	24.51
215.	Sugar	24.38
216.	Clothes dryers	23.95
217.	Bathroom linens	23.90
218.	Sweetrolls, coffee cakes, doughnuts	23.73
219.	Cooking stoves, ovens	23.67
220.	Cream	23.58
221.	Checking accounts, other bank service charges	23.10
222.	Bicycles	21.69
223.	Other alcoholic beverages at home	21.40
224.	Hearing aids	21.23
225.	Photographer fees	21.12
226.	Nonclothing laundry and dry cleaning, sent out	21.09
227.	Recreation expenses on trips	20.99
228.	Canned fruits	20.35
229.	Automobile service clubs	20.09

230.	Laundry and cleaning equipment	$19.59
231.	Outdoor furniture	19.36
232.	Shaving products	19.18
233.	Vegetable juices	18.98
234.	Tableware, nonelectric kitchenware	18.89
235.	Intercity train fares	18.88
236.	Nonelectric cookware	18.86
237.	Peanut butter	18.68
238.	Nondairy cream and imitation milk	18.59
239.	Dried vegetables	18.22
240.	Local transportation on trips	17.81
241.	Olives, pickles, relishes	17.46
242.	Gifts of stocks, bonds, and mutual funds to members of other households	17.16
243.	Fresh fruit juice	17.06
244.	Musical instruments and accessories	16.80
245.	Dishwashers (built-in), garbage disposals, range hoods	16.61
246.	Books and supplies for elementary and high school	16.25
247.	Floor coverings	16.22
248.	Prepared flour mixes	16.18
249.	Electric floor-cleaning equipment	16.07
250.	Test preparation, tutoring services	15.86
251.	Computer accessories	15.85
252.	Rental of video cassettes, tapes, discs, films	15.72
253.	Maintenance and repair services, renter	15.71
254.	Nonalcoholic beverages (except carbonated, coffee, fruit-flavored drinks, and tea) and ice	15.36
255.	Appliance repair, including at service center	15.36
256.	Sports drinks	15.12
257.	Watches	15.09
258.	Computer software	15.04
259.	Satellite radio service	14.83
260.	Tenant's insurance	14.74
261.	Window coverings	14.64
262.	Prepared desserts	14.29
263.	Luggage	13.79
264.	Digital book readers	13.62
265.	Security services, owner	13.56
266.	Infants' equipment	13.42
267.	Pies, tarts, turnovers	13.41
268.	Cemetery lots, vaults, and maintenance fees	13.16
269.	Whiskey at home	12.93
270.	Living room tables	12.92
271.	Rental of party supplies for catered affairs	12.63
272.	Closet and storage items	12.60
273.	Intercity bus fares	11.96
274.	Vehicle inspection	11.85
275.	Hand tools	11.79
276.	Compact discs, records, and audio tapes	11.78
277.	Driver's license	11.64
278.	Taxi fares and limousine service	11.36
279.	Camping equipment	11.06
280.	Newspapers and magazines, nonsubscription	10.88
281.	Microwave ovens	10.55
282.	Streamed and downloaded audio	10.39
283.	Electric personal care appliances	10.39
284.	Lamb, organ meats, and others	10.19
285.	Shopping club membership fees	10.16
286.	Curtains and draperies	9.88
287.	Voice over IP	9.64

288.	Infants' furniture	$9.59
289.	Flour	9.36
290.	Photo processing	9.15
291.	Phone cards	9.00
292.	Hair accessories	8.92
293.	Parking at owned home	8.87
294.	Portable heating and cooling equipment	8.84
295.	Stamp and coin collecting	8.80
296.	China and other dinnerware	8.76
297.	Margarine	8.74
298.	Material for making clothes	8.74
299.	Coal, wood, and other fuels	8.72
300.	Dried fruits	8.71
301.	Sewing materials for household items	8.48
302.	Internet services away from home	8.25
303.	Kitchen and dining room linens	8.15
304.	Miscellaneous video equipment	8.08
305.	Glassware	7.94
306.	Repairs and rentals of lawn and garden equipment, hand and power tools, etc.	7.90
307.	Vocational and technical school tuition	7.66
308.	Docking and landing fees	7.45
309.	Personal digital audio players	7.41
310.	Vacation clubs	7.38
311.	VCRs and video disc players	7.35
312.	Bread and cracker products	7.31
313.	Frozen fruits	7.16
314.	Maintenance and repair materials, renter	7.12
315.	Live entertainment for catered affairs	6.48
316.	Rental of recreational vehicles	6.11
317.	Apparel alteration, repair, and tailoring services	6.03
318.	Office furniture for home use	6.02
319.	Global positioning system devices	5.66
320.	Frozen fruit juices	5.55
321.	Repair of computer systems for nonbusiness use	5.52
322.	Streamed and downloaded video	5.35
323.	Medical equipment for general use	5.16
324.	Window air conditioners	4.95
325.	Artificial sweeteners	4.91
326.	Nonclothing laundry and dry cleaning, coin-operated	4.79
327.	Watch and jewelry repair	4.72
328.	Personal digital assistants	4.70
329.	Water sports equipment	4.45
330.	Rental of furniture	4.44
331.	Towing charges	4.37
332.	Water-softening service	4.30
333.	Sewing patterns and notions	4.20
334.	Winter sports equipment	4.19
335.	Slipcovers and decorative pillows	3.94
336.	Applications, games, ringtones for handheld devices	3.86
337.	Portable memory	3.76
338.	Business equipment for home use	3.63
339.	Online gaming services	3.51
340.	Supportive and convalescent medical equipment	3.48
341.	Delivery services	3.43
342.	Safe deposit box rental	3.36
343.	Video game software	3.26
344.	Reupholstering and furniture repair	3.21
345.	Repair of TV, radio, and sound equipment	3.09
346.	Septic tank cleaning	2.95

347.	Flatware	$2.93
348.	Credit card memberships	2.92
349.	Deductions for railroad retirement	2.89
350.	Adult diapers	2.86
351.	Playground equipment	2.84
352.	Wigs and hairpieces	2.82
353.	Plastic dinnerware	2.68
354.	Smoking accessories	2.68
355.	Sewing machines	2.54
356.	Fireworks	2.46
357.	Global positioning services	2.06
358.	Silver serving pieces	2.04
359.	Rental and repair of miscellaneous sports equipment	1.86
360.	Pinball, electronic video games	1.78
361.	Smoke alarms	1.75
362.	Rental and repair of musical instruments	1.70
363.	Clothing rental	1.69
364.	Rental of medical equipment	1.53
365.	Shoe repair and other shoe services	1.52
366.	Appliance rental	1.50
367.	Satellite dishes	1.24
368.	School bus	1.15
369.	Other serving pieces	1.04
370.	Installation of television sets	0.74
371.	Books and supplies for vocational and technical schools	0.71
372.	Clothing storage	0.70
373.	Rental of office equipment for nonbusiness use	0.68
374.	Rental of supportive and convalescent medical equipment	0.68
375.	Telephone answering devices	0.59
376.	Dating services	0.50
377.	Installation of computer	0.44
378.	Repair and rental of photographic equipment	0.39
379.	Books and supplies for day care and nursery	0.38

Source: Calculations by New Strategist based on the Bureau of Labor Statistics' 2012 Consumer Expenditure Survey

Glossary

age The age of the reference person.

alcoholic beverages Includes beer and ale, wine, whiskey, gin, vodka, rum, and other alcoholic beverages.

annual spending The annual amount spent per household. The Bureau of Labor Statistics calculates the annual average for all households in a segment, not just for those that purchased an item. The averages are calculated by integrating the results of the diary (weekly) and interview (quarterly) portions of the Consumer Expenditure Survey. For items purchased by most households—such as bread—average annual spending figures are a fairly accurate account of actual spending. For products and services purchased by few households during a year's time—such as cars—the average annual amount spent is much less than what purchasers spend.

apparel, accessories, and related services Includes the following:

• *men's and boys' apparel* Includes coats, jackets, sweaters, vests, sport coats, tailored jackets, slacks, shorts and short sets, sportswear, shirts, underwear, nightwear, hosiery, uniforms, and other accessories.

• *women's and girls' apparel* Includes coats, jackets, furs, sport coats, tailored jackets, sweaters, vests, blouses, shirts, dresses, dungarees, culottes, slacks, shorts, sportswear, underwear, nightwear, uniforms, hosiery, and other accessories.

• *infants' apparel* Includes coats, jackets, snowsuits, underwear, diapers, dresses, crawlers, sleeping garments, hosiery, footwear, and other accessories for children.

• *footwear* Includes articles such as shoes, slippers, boots, and other similar items. It excludes footwear for babies and footwear used for sports such as bowling or golf shoes.

• *other apparel products and services* Includes material for making clothes, shoe repair, alterations and sewing patterns and notions, clothing rental, clothing storage, dry cleaning, sent-out laundry, watches, jewelry, and repairs to watches and jewelry.

baby boom Americans born between 1946 and 1964.

cash contributions Includes cash contributed to persons or organizations outside the consumer unit including court-ordered alimony, child support payments, support for college students, and contributions to religious, educational, charitable, or political organizations.

consumer unit (1) All members of a household who are related by blood, marriage, adoption, or other legal arrangements; (2) a person living alone or sharing a household with others or living as a roomer in a private home or lodging house or in permanent living quarters in a hotel or motel, but who is financially independent; or (3) two or more persons living together who pool their income to make joint expenditure decisions. Financial independence is determined by the three major expense categories: housing, food, and other living expenses. To be considered financially independent, at least two of the three major expense categories have to be provided by the respondent. For convenience, called household in the text of this report.

consumer unit, composition of The classification of interview households by type according to (1) relationship of other household members to the reference person; (2) age of the children of the reference person; and (3) combination of relationship to the reference person and age of the children. Stepchildren and adopted children are included with the reference person's own children.

earner A consumer unit member aged 14 or older who worked at least one week during the 12 months prior to the interview date.

education Includes tuition, fees, books, supplies, and equipment for public and private nursery schools, elementary and high schools, colleges and universities, and other schools.

entertainment Includes the following:

• *fees and admissions* Includes fees for participant sports; admissions to sporting events, movies, concerts, plays; health, swimming, tennis, and country club memberships, and other social recreational and fraternal organizations; recreational lessons or instructions; and recreational expenses on trips.

• *audio and visual equipment and services* Includes television sets; radios; cable TV; tape recorders and players; video cassettes, tapes, and discs; video cassette recorders and video disc players; video game hardware and software; personal digital audio players; streaming and downloading audio and video; sound components; CDs, records, and tapes; musical instruments; and rental and repair of TV and sound equipment.

• *pets, toys, hobbies, and playground equipment* Includes pet food, pet services, veterinary expenses, toys, games, hobbies, and playground equipment.

• *other entertainment equipment and services* Includes indoor exercise equipment, athletic shoes, bicycles, trailers, campers, camping equipment, rental of campers and trailers, hunting and fishing equipment, sports equipment, winter sports equipment, water sports equipment, boats, boat motors and boat trailers, rental of boats, landing and docking fees, rental and repair of sports equipment, photographic equipment, film, photo processing, photographer fees, repair and rental of photo equipment, fireworks, pinball and electronic video games.

expenditure The transaction cost including excise and sales taxes of goods and services acquired during the survey period. The full cost of each purchase is recorded even though full payment may not have been made at the date of purchase. Expenditure estimates include gifts. Excluded from expenditures are purchases or portions of purchases directly assignable to business purposes and periodic credit or installment payments on goods and services already acquired.

federal income tax Includes federal income tax withheld in the survey year to pay for income earned in survey year plus additional tax paid in survey year to cover any underpayment or underwithholding of tax in the year prior to the survey.

financial products and services Includes accounting fees, legal fees, union dues, professional dues and fees, other occupational expenses, funerals, cemetery lots, dating services, shopping club memberships, and unclassified fees and personal services.

food Includes the following:

• *food at home* Refers to the total expenditures for food at grocery stores or other food stores during the interview period. It is calculated by multiplying the number of visits to a grocery or other food store by the average amount spent per visit. It excludes the purchase of nonfood items.

• *food away from home* Includes all meals (breakfast, lunch, brunch, and dinner) at restaurants, carry-outs, and vending machines, including tips, plus meals as pay, special catered affairs such as weddings, bar mitzvahs, and confirmations, and meals away from home on trips.

generation X Americans born between 1965 and 1976. Also known as the baby-bust generation.

gifts for people in other households Includes gift expenditures for people living in other consumer units. The amount spent on gifts is also included in individual product and service categories.

health care Includes the following:

• *health insurance* Includes health maintenance plans (HMOs), Blue Cross/Blue Shield, commercial health insurance, Medicare, Medicare supplemental insurance, long-term care insurance, and other health insurance.

• *medical services* Includes hospital room and services, physicians' services, services of a practitioner other than a physician, eye and dental care, lab tests, X-rays, nursing, therapy services, care in convalescent or nursing home, and other medical care.

• *drugs* Includes prescription and nonprescription drugs, internal and respiratory over-the-counter drugs.

• *medical supplies* Includes eyeglasses and contact lenses, topicals and dressings, antiseptics, bandages, cotton, first aid kits, contraceptives; medical equipment for general use such as syringes, ice bags, thermometers, vaporizers, heating pads; supportive or convalescent medical equipment such as hearing aids, braces, canes, crutches, and walkers.

Hispanic origin The self-identified Hispanic origin of the consumer unit reference person. All consumer units are included in one of two Hispanic origin groups based on the reference person's Hispanic origin: Hispanic or non-Hispanic. Hispanics may be of any race.

household According to the Census Bureau, all the people who occupy a household. A group of unrelated people who share a housing unit as roommates or unmarried partners is also counted as a household. Households do not include group quarters such as college dormitories, prisons, or nursing homes. A household may contain more than one consumer unit. The terms "household" and "consumer unit" are used interchangeably in this report.

household furnishings and equipment Includes the following:

• *household textiles* Includes bathroom, kitchen, dining room, and other linens, curtains and drapes, slipcovers and decorative pillows, and sewing materials.

• *furniture* Includes living room, dining room, kitchen, bedroom, nursery, porch, lawn, and other outdoor furniture.

• *carpet, rugs, and other floor coverings* Includes installation and replacement of wall-to-wall carpets, room-size rugs, and other soft floor coverings.

• *major appliances* Includes refrigerators, freezers, dishwashers, stoves, ovens, garbage disposals, vacuum cleaners, microwave ovens, air-conditioners, sewing machines, washing machines, clothes dryers, and floor-cleaning equipment.

• *small appliances and miscellaneous housewares* Includes small electrical kitchen appliances, portable heating and cooling equipment, china and other dinnerware, flatware, glassware, silver and other serving pieces, nonelectric cookware, and plastic dinnerware. Excludes personal care appliances.

• *miscellaneous household equipment* Includes computer hardware and software, luggage, lamps and other lighting fixtures, window coverings, clocks, lawn mowers and gardening equipment, hand and power tools, telephone answering devices, personal digital assistants, Internet services away from home, office equipment for home use, fresh flowers and house plants, rental of furniture, closet and storage items, household decorative items, infants' equipment, outdoor equipment, smoke alarms, other household appliances, and small miscellaneous furnishing.

household services Includes the following:

• *personal services* Includes baby sitting, day care, and care of elderly and handicapped persons.

• *other household services* Includes computer information services; housekeeping services; gardening and lawn care services; coin-operated laundry and dry-cleaning of household textiles; termite and pest control products; moving, storage, and freight expenses; repair of household appliances and other household equipment; reupholstering and furniture repair; rental and repair of lawn and gardening tools, and rental of other household equipment.

housekeeping supplies Includes soaps, detergents, other laundry cleaning products, cleansing and toilet tissue, paper towels, napkins, and miscellaneous household products; lawn and garden supplies, postage, stationery, stationery supplies, and gift wrap.

housing tenure "Owner" includes households living in their own homes, cooperatives, condominiums, or townhouses. "Renter" includes households paying rent as well as families living rent free in lieu of wages.

income before taxes The total money earnings and selected money receipts accruing to a consumer unit during the 12 months prior to the interview date. Income includes the following components:

• *wages and salaries* Includes total money earnings for all members of the consumer unit aged 14 or older from all jobs, including civilian wages and salaries, Armed Forces pay and allowances, piece-rate payments, commissions, tips, National Guard or Reserve pay (received for training periods), and cash bonuses before deductions for taxes, pensions, union dues, etc.

• *self-employment income* Includes net business and farm income, which consists of net income (gross receipts minus operating expenses) from a profession or unincorporated business or from the operation of a farm by an owner, tenant, or sharecropper. If the business or farm is a partnership, only an appropriate share of net income is recorded. Losses are also recorded.

• *Social Security, private and government retirement* Includes payments by the federal government made under retirement, survivor, and disability insurance programs to retired persons, dependents of deceased insured workers, or to disabled workers; and private pensions or retirement benefits received by retired persons or their survivors, either directly or through an insurance company.

• *interest, dividends, rental income, and other property income* Includes interest income on savings or bonds; payments made by a corporation to its stockholders, periodic receipts from estates or trust funds; net income or loss from the rental of property, real estate, or farms, and net income or loss from roomers or boarders.

• *unemployment and workers' compensation and veterans' benefit.* Includes income from unemployment compensation and workers compensation, and veterans' payments including educational benefits but excluding military retirement.

• *public assistance, supplemental security income, and food stamps* Includes public assistance or welfare, including money received from job training grants; supplemental security income paid by federal, state, and local welfare agencies to low-income persons who are aged 65 or older, blind, or disabled; and the value of food stamps obtained.

• *regular contributions for support* Includes alimony and child support as well as any regular contributions from persons outside the consumer unit.

• *other income* Includes money income from care of foster children, cash scholarships, fellowships, or stipends not based on working; and meals and rent as pay.

indexed spending Indexed spending figures compare the spending of particular demographic segments with that of the average household. To compute an index, the amount spent on an item by a demographic segment is divided by the amount spent on the item by the average household. That figure is then multiplied by 100. An index of 100 is the average for all households. An index of 125 means average spending by households in a segment is 25 percent above average (100 plus 25). An index of 75 means average spending by households in a segment is 25 percent below average (100 minus 25). Indexed spending figures identify the consumer units that spend the most on a product or service.

life and other personal insurance Includes premiums from whole life and term insurance; endowments; income and other life insurance; mortgage guarantee insurance; mortgage life insurance; premiums for personal life liability, accident and disability; and other non–health insurance other than homes and vehicles.

market share The market share is the percentage of total household spending on an item that is accounted for by a demographic segment. Market shares are calculated by dividing a demographic segment's total spending on an item by the total spending of all households on the item. Total spending on an item for all households is calculated by multiplying average spending by the total number of households. Total spending on an item for each demographic segment is calculated by multiplying the segment's average spending by the number of households in the segment. Market shares reveal the demographic segments that account for the largest share of spending on a product or service.

millennial generation Americans born between 1977 and 1994.

occupation The occupation in which the reference person received the most earnings during the survey period. The occupational categories follow those of the Census of Population. Categories shown in the tables include the following:

• *self-employed* Includes all occupational categories; the reference person is self-employed in own business, professional practice, or farm.

• *wage and salary earners, managers and professionals* Includes executives, administrators, managers, and professional specialties such as architects, engineers, natural and social scientists, lawyers, teachers, writers, health diagnosis and treatment workers, entertainers, and athletes.

• *wage and salary earners, technical, sales, and clerical workers* Includes technicians and related support workers; sales representatives, sales workers, cashiers, and sales-related occupations; and administrative support, including clerical.

• *retired* People who did not work either full- or part-time during the survey period.

owner *See* housing tenure.

pensions and Social Security Includes all Social Security contributions paid by employees; employees' contributions to railroad retirement, government retirement and private pensions programs; retirement programs for self-employed.

personal care Includes products for the hair, oral hygiene products, shaving needs, cosmetics, bath products, suntan lotions, hand creams, electric personal care appliances, incontinence products, other personal care products, personal care services such as hair care services (haircuts, bleaching, tinting, coloring, conditioning treatments, permanents, press, and curls), styling and other services for wigs and hairpieces, body massages or slenderizing treatments, facials, manicures, pedicures, shaves, electrolysis.

quarterly spending Quarterly spending data are collected in the interview portion of the Consumer Expenditure Survey. Quarterly spending tables show the percentage of households that purchased an item during an average quarter, and the amount spent during the quarter on the item by purchasers. Not all items are included in the interview portion of the Consumer Expenditure Survey.

reading Includes subscriptions for newspapers, magazines, and books through book clubs; purchase of single-copy newspapers and magazines, books, and encyclopedias and other reference books.

reference person The first member mentioned by the respondent when asked to "Start with the name of the person or one of the persons who owns or rents the home." It is with respect to this person that the relationship of other consumer unit members is determined. Also called the householder or head of household.

region Consumer units are classified according to their address at the time of their participation in the survey. The four major census regions of the United States are the following state groupings:

• *Northeast* Connecticut, Maine, Massachusetts, New Hampshire, New Jersey, New York, Pennsylvania, Rhode Island, and Vermont.

• *Midwest* Illinois, Indiana, Iowa, Kansas, Michigan, Minnesota, Mississippi, Nebraska, North Dakota, Ohio, South Dakota, and Wisconsin.

• *South* Alabama, Arkansas, Delaware, District of Columbia, Florida, Georgia, Kentucky, Louisiana, Maryland, Mississippi, North Carolina, Oklahoma, South Carolina, Tennessee, Texas, Virginia, and West Virginia.

• *West* Alaska, Arizona, California, Colorado, Hawaii, Idaho, Minnesota, Nevada, New Mexico, Oregon, Utah, Washington, and Wyoming.

renter *See* housing tenure.

shelter Includes the following:

• *owned dwellings* Includes interest on mortgages, property taxes and insurance, refinancing and prepayment charges, ground rent, expenses for property management and security, homeowner's insurance, fire insurance and extended coverage, landscaping expenses for repairs and maintenance contracted out (including periodic maintenance and service contracts), and expenses of materials for owner-performed repairs and maintenance for dwellings used or maintained by the consumer unit, but not dwellings maintained for business or rent.

• *rented dwellings* Includes rent paid for dwellings, rent received as pay, parking fees, maintenance, and other expenses.

• *other lodging* Includes all expenses for vacation homes, school, college, hotels, motels, cottages, trailer camps, and other lodging while out of town.

• *utilities, fuels, and public services* Includes natural gas, electricity, fuel oil, coal, bottled gas, wood, other fuels; residential telephone service, cell phone service, phone cards; water, garbage, trash collection; sewerage maintenance, septic tank cleaning; and other public services.

size of consumer unit The number of people whose usual place of residence at the time of the interview is in the consumer unit.

state and local income taxes Includes state and local income taxes withheld in the survey year to pay for income earned in survey year plus additional taxes paid in the survey year to cover any underpayment or underwithholding of taxes in the year prior to the survey.

tobacco and smoking supplies Includes cigarettes, cigars, snuff, loose smoking tobacco, chewing tobacco, and smoking accessories such as cigarette or cigar holders, pipes, flints, lighters, pipe cleaners, and other smoking products and accessories.

transportation Includes the following:

• *vehicle purchases* (net outlay) Includes the net outlay (purchase price minus trade-in value) on new and used domestic and imported cars and trucks and other vehicles, including motorcycles and private planes.

• *gasoline and motor oil* Includes gasoline, diesel fuel, and motor oil.

• *other vehicle expenses* Includes vehicle finance charges, maintenance and repairs, vehicle insurance, and vehicle rental licenses and other charges.

• *vehicle finance charges* Includes the dollar amount of interest paid for a loan contracted for the purchase of vehicles described above.

• *maintenance and repairs* Includes tires, batteries, tubes, lubrication, filters, coolant, additives, brake and transmission fluids, oil change, brake adjustment and repair, front-end alignment, wheel balancing, steering repair, shock absorber replacement, clutch and transmission repair, electrical system repair, repair to cooling system, drive train repair, drive shaft and rear-end repair, tire repair, vehicle video equipment, other maintenance and services, and auto repair policies.

• *vehicle insurance* Includes the premium paid for insuring cars, trucks, and other vehicles.

• *vehicle rental, licenses, and other charges* Includes leased and rented cars, trucks, motorcycles, and aircraft, inspection fees, state and local registration, drivers' license fees, parking fees, towing charges, tolls on trips, and global positioning services.

• *public transportation* Includes fares for mass transit, buses, trains, airlines, taxis, private school buses, and fares paid on trips for trains, boats, taxis, buses, and trains.

weekly spending Weekly spending data are collected in the diary portion of the Consumer Expenditure Survey. The data show the percentage of households that purchased an item during the average week, and the amount spent per week on the item by purchasers. Not all items are included in the diary portion of the Consumer Expenditure Survey.